Laughing with Sarah

Thoughts on the Journey with God

by Gene Jennings

Late Night Press

ISBN 978-0-578-01963-5

First Printing, April 2009

Cover designed by Matt McMeans of www.kruhu.com

Additional copies of this book can be found at
www.laughingwithsarah.com or www.genejennings.com

Late Night Press, North Augusta, SC

Printed in the U.S.A.

Dedication

Dedicated to my dad, David Jennings, whose life exemplifies his passion for the Bible.

Foreword

You may not want to know this, but since most people don't read forewords, I'll say it right here. This is a book of sermons. Messages I've presented to congregations over the years that I have particularly liked. I wouldn't say that it's a greatest hits collection. I don't have enough of those to constitute a book. I also wouldn't say it's thematic since they are in no particular order and don't necessarily carry a common thread – with one exception. It's about the journey.

Following Christ is a journey. It's an adventure. I've been on this journey for over three decades now, and I'm sorry to say that I haven't perfected it yet. There was a time years ago, when I was naïve and ignorant, when I thought that I would be able to reach the mountaintop of spiritual maturity and bask in its glow and show the masses Christian perfection.

I've since learned that it doesn't work that way.

Following Jesus is a series of mountaintops and valleys. Most of the time, we are somewhere in between. There are times when God shows us something so unbelievable that we, like Sarah, laugh at the ridiculousness of it all. There are also times when he moves us so profoundly that we can do nothing but stare in awe. This is a collection of messages turned essays that will trigger thoughts, bring wisdom, and give practical insights to help you along the way - wherever it is you may find yourself – on the journey with God.

Thanks to Vickie Long for doing a wonderful job of editing and Karin Soderstrom for typing some of my old notes into a 21st century word-processing program.

Thanks also to my beautiful bride of over 25 years, Beth. She encourages me to persist at this writing thing.

Sermons are like research papers. They include original thoughts, along with quotes, statistics, and stories gathered from other sources. I have cited all of the sources possible. Where I've omitted some, please know that it is not intentional.

Contents

1

The Thanksgiving Killer

Thanksgiving dinner is one of the greatest meals of the year. A typical spread for us includes turkey, honey ham, green bean casserole, sweet potato casserole, rice and gravy, cream corn, dressing, potato salad, macaroni and cheese, and broccoli casserole. For dessert, we have red velvet cake, pecan pie, coconut cake, fudge, and chocolate chip cookies. When I walk in the kitchen to see all of the work that went into the meal, it looks like the first three rows at the end of a Gallagher show.

After pigging out, we sit back stuffed, miserable, and grateful for all of the incredible food. We visit with relatives while keeping our eyes on the football game on TV and reflect on the past and dream about the future. We enjoy seeing family and friends that we don't often see. Later that night, I go to bed grateful for all the blessings I have.

Then the Thanksgiving killer arrives.

Black Friday - the day after Thanksgiving when the Christmas shopping season officially begins. Stores open at four AM. Consumers camp out at the malls. Shoppers and store employees are trampled. A shopping tragedy will be on the six o'clock news. Somewhere someone will do something stupid and someone else will pay for it.

Why is Black Friday the Thanksgiving killer? Because on Thanksgiving Day, we thought about all that we have and we were grateful. But on the day after Thanksgiving through the rest of the holidays, we focus not on what we have, but on what we want.

The Thanksgiving killer is the Christmas commercialism that says we need more. Just when we have a day to be thankful for all of our blessings, the Thanksgiving killers show up and tell us that we will not be happy until we have something more.

Someone wrote, "Half the world is unhappy because it can't have the things that are making the other half unhappy."

Author Steve Brown wrote, "The most unhappy person in the world is not someone who didn't get what he or she wanted. The most unhappy person is the one who got what he or she wanted and then found out that it wasn't as wonderful as expected. The secret of a happy life is not to get what you want but to live with what you've got. Most of us spend our lives concentrating on what we don't have instead of thanking God for what we do have."[1]

Our problem is that we are looking at the Christmas advertisements focusing on what we want rather than looking at our photo albums and rejoicing in what we have! It's the grass-is-always-greener-on-the-other-side syndrome. We always want more. I am as guilty as anyone.

For years I wanted a motorcycle. I wrote it down as one of my life goals back in the early '90's. I used to talk about that "one day" when I would finally own a motorcycle. I used to drive my poor wife crazy. I would see other people riding their motorcycles on a beautiful day and think, "Man, I wish I had a bike! If only I had a motorcycle, not a big one, not an expensive one, but just an average size bike in good condition that I can afford and ride on pretty days. If I had one my life would be complete." Well, guess what? I finally bought a motorcycle. It's been fun...but it didn't make my life complete. In fact, I wished I had gotten a bigger one, so I bought another one a year later.

We always want more.

I read about an airline pilot with a peculiar habit. Whenever he took off from his hometown of Minneapolis, he would ask the copilot to take the controls. Then he would stare intently out the window for a few moments. Finally, the copilot's curiosity got the best of him, so he asked, "What do you always look at down there?" "See that river?" the pilot asked. "I used to fish that river when I was a kid. Whenever a plane flew over, I would watch it until it disappeared and wish that I could be the pilot." With a sigh he added, "Now I wish I could be back down there fishing."

We just can't seem to find satisfaction and contentment. There is always something more, something else, something more important. Because we live with this mindset, it is easy to forget to be thankful. We allow our consumer mentality and desire for more to kill the need to be thankful.

If a stranger unfamiliar with our culture dropped into America for the first time, would the word "thankful" be one of the first adjectives he would use to describe us? Probably not.

We always want just a little bit more.

If our jobs were a little different...

If our houses were a little bigger...

If our neighborhood was a little nicer...

If our spouses would only do this...

If our families would only understand this...

If our boss would only...

If whatever...

There seems to be a law of inverse blessing. The more people have the less outwardly thankful they become.

Martin Luther said, "If God were more close-handed with his gifts, we would be more thankful. The greater God's gifts and works, the less they are regarded."

What if a cloud shrouded the earth so that we could not see the stars or planets? And what if one night every ten years that cloud disappeared so that we could see the stars and the planets? What would you do? You would go out that night and take in the wonder of the universe. It would be an exciting event! But because they are there every night, we barely give them a look.

We are so blessed in this country that we have become spoiled little rich kids. We don't stop and consider our blessings and thank God enough. A native of a third world country came to the United States for the first time, and as he was riding through a subdivision, he saw a car backing out of a garage, and he observed out loud, "You all have houses for your cars?"

We don't always realize how blessed we are and how affluent we are as American citizens.

If you have food in the refrigerator, clothes on your back, a roof over your head, and a place to sleep, then you're richer than 75% of the world. If you have money in the bank, in your wallet, and spare change in a dish someplace, then you're among the 8% of the world's wealthy.

Not until things are taken away do we sometimes begin to appreciate what God has given us. Take Helen Keller, for example, who once said, "I have often thought it would be a blessing if each human being were stricken blind and deaf for a few days at some time during his early adult life. It would make him more appreciative of sight and the joys of sound."

Look at what the apostle Paul wrote in the New
Testament book of Philippians:

> I have learned to be content whatever the
> circumstances. I know what it is to be in need, and I
> know what it is to have plenty. I have learned the
> secret of being content in any and every situation,
> whether well fed or hungry, whether living in plenty or
> in want. I can do everything through him who gives me
> strength ... And my God will meet all your needs
> according to his glorious riches in Christ Jesus.
> (Philippians 4:11-13, 19)

Paul wrote these words from prison at a time when he
was held under arrest for spreading the message of Jesus
Christ.

We need to learn the secret of contentment from Paul.
We need to learn the art of gratefulness and thanksgiving for
the many blessings that we have. If only we would realize that
we already have everything that we need. Do you know that?
You have everything you need.

> His divine power has given us everything we need for
> life and godliness through our knowledge of him who
> called us by his own glory and goodness. (2 Peter 1:3)

The Lord is my shepherd, I have everything I need.
(Psalm 23:1, NLT)

Everything - no other conquests are necessary. No shopping trips required. No further accumulation needed. Each of us can honestly say, "I've got a lot to be thankful for." But the Christ follower says, "I have everything I need in Jesus Christ, and that can never ever be taken away."

Not just some things. Not just most things. Not even all but one thing. No. He has given us everything we need for life. Everything we need for a fulfilling life! How could I ask for more?

How do we get this blessing? Note the second half of the verse in 2 Peter: "through our knowledge of him." As you get to know God, as you grow closer to him, as you understand what he has done, you will discover that he has provided you with everything you need.

What has God given us? What do we need to know about God? Why should we be thankful?

A Thanksgiving Psalm of David

Blessed is he whose transgressions are forgiven, whose sins are covered. Blessed is the man whose sin the Lord does not count against him and in whose spirit is no deceit. When I kept silent, my bones wasted away through my groaning all day long. For day and night your hand was heavy upon me; my strength was sapped as in the heat of summer. Then I acknowledged my sin to you and did not cover up my iniquity. I said, "I will confess my transgressions to the Lord "- and you forgave the guilt of my sin. Therefore let everyone who is godly pray to you while you may be found; surely when the mighty waters rise, they will not reach him. You are my hiding place; you will protect me from trouble and surround me with songs of deliverance. I will instruct you and teach you in the way you should go; I will counsel you and watch over you. Do not be like the horse or the mule, which have no understanding but must be controlled by bit and bridle or they will not come to you. Many are the woes of the wicked, but the Lord's unfailing love surrounds the man who trusts in him. Rejoice in the Lord and be glad, you righteous; sing, all you who are upright in heart! (Psalm 32)

David expresses at least five blessings for which we should be thankful.

Forgiveness

David says that God's forgiveness is complete. Our sins are covered. God looks at you no matter how filthy your past may be and says, "I've got you covered." There are so many people that think they are too dirty for God. You are not too dirty for him. He loves you and cares deeply for you. He made you. You are his creation, and you cannot do anything to change his love for you.

Don't go through life with the heavy burden of sin on your back. Sin wears you down. David said it wasted away at his body. It caused him to groan and be in spiritual misery. It sapped his strength like a hot summer afternoon. It took away what little spiritual energy he had.

But when you acknowledge your faults to God, when you uncover your sins, there is forgiveness. With forgiveness, there is freedom. If you've never experienced God's forgiveness, you'll never believe how the weight of sin can be lifted off.

An old song says, "Burdens are lifted at Calvary" and it is true. When you realize that you can give all of your sins, faults, and shortcomings to Christ, it is the most liberating thing you can ever experience.

Thank God for forgiveness.

Availability

Because our sin is covered by Christ's sacrifice on the cross, God is available to us. This is the essence of the cross. Jesus Christ took upon himself the sin of the world. He took on the sins of the past, the sins of the present, and the sins of the future. By taking on the sin of the world, he paid the ultimate price of death so that we could be forgiven and so that God could be available to us.

David wrote, "Therefore let everyone who is godly pray to you while you may be found" (v. 6). You might ask, "Gene, this says everyone who is godly. I'm not godly." If you have experienced God's forgiveness and accepted Christ's death on your behalf, you are. You are clean. You are pure. Therefore, you are godly. I didn't say that you are God, but godly, which means "God-like."

The Bible tells us that when we allow God to cover our sins, then God sees us as pure and holy just as he sees Christ himself. In that respect, you are godly when you experience his forgiveness and because you have experienced his forgiveness, you can have an eternal relationship with him. He is available to you forever!

That is definitely something to be thankful for! Thank God that he has given us his availability. This blows the theology of the deist. A deist believes that God has no control or input into his creation. But this tells us that we can communicate with and have a relationship with God.

Have you ever had a friend say, "Call me anytime you need me." Did you ever take them up on it? Weren't you grateful that you had that friend who was available to help you in your time of need? That's how God is. He is available 24/7. He wants to be your constant companion and resource if you will just let him. Thank God that he makes himself available to us.

Protection

David also adds that God has given us his protection. He describes God as his hiding place. Do you remember when you were a kid trying to go to sleep in your bed at night, but you were afraid? You were afraid that the boogeyman or some monster from underneath your bed was going to get you? I remember thinking, "Okay, I know there's a monster under my bed, and it's just a matter of time before he comes up and gets me. So I'm going to get out of here before he gets a chance. I'd lie still like I was asleep to try to fool the monster. I was working on the element of surprise. At just the right time, when I got enough courage, I would jump out of the bed and run as fast as I could out of my room, across the hall, and fly like Superman in between my mama and daddy in their bed.

There was nothing like the protection of my big ole daddy. The boogeyman under my bed would have to wait another night because I was in my hiding place. I was under the protection of a 6'4", 250 lb. creature named David Jennings and that monster was no match for him!

God grants us protection both spiritually and physically. I have no doubt that God protected me many, many times when I was doing some stupid things early in my life. Now that I have my own children, I rely on God's supernatural protection even more!

Thank God that he provides protection for us. He protects us from ourselves as well as other people, the elements, even our spiritual enemies.

Instruction

David says that God will instruct you and teach you in the way you should go. He will counsel you and watch over you. What a great gift!

What would you say if someone came up to you and said, "I've got some great news! Because I care for you so much I was able to swing a deal on your behalf. I'm going to get Dr. James Dobson to be your personal family counselor on call 24 hours a day, free! If you ever have a problem or question, Dr. Dobson will personally come to your house and help you raise your family. Then for your finances, Warren Buffet, the guru of Wall Street, at no charge to you, has agreed to meet with you each week and help you build a phenomenal portfolio, and your money worries will be over. To help you with your spiritual life, Rick Warren, voted America's most influential pastor by *Christianity Today* magazine and the author of the bestselling book *The Purpose Driven Life*, will meet with you each morning to get your day started off right with God."

How would you respond? "Wow, I can't go wrong with great teachers like that involved in every day of my life."

Well, guess what? You have an even better teacher and counselor than that! You have the God of the universe as your own personal teacher every second of every day! He will teach you and tell you which direction to go. He will counsel you and look over your shoulder and guide you throughout your entire life.

What a blessing! Thank God that the Creator of the universe gives us his undivided attention at our beckoning call! All you have to do is ask him.

Unfailing Love

Finally, David reminds us that God has given us his unfailing love. "Many are the woes of the wicked, but the Lord's unfailing love surrounds the man who trusts in him" (v. 10).

Did you know that one of your deepest desires is love? But not just a temporary, finicky, sporadic, wishy-washy kind of love. You deeply desire an unending, never failing kind of love. Everyone in this world wants this kind of love. How do I know that? Because the Bible says so. Proverbs 19:22 says, "What a man desires is unfailing love." What God offers you is his unfailing love.

Do you know that God has loved you longer than anyone else? He knew you long before your family and friends knew you. He loved you years ago, decades ago, centuries ago. He couldn't wait for you to get here so that he could show you his love. When you were born, God thought, "Great! Now I can finally grow him up and show him my love!"

God's love for you is never ending, and it breaks his heart when you don't love him back. You were planned for God's pleasure. One of our life's purposes is to know God's love and love him back.

Have you ever seen something that was never ending? Scientists say that it is impossible to create a perpetual motion machine. You may be able to make a machine that can stay in motion for a long time, but eventually it will fail. My grandfather was a tinkerer, an inventor, and somewhat of an amateur scientist. He knew that perpetual motion machines had been tried and tried for centuries, but he tried to make one anyway. Many times I would stop by his house, and he would be in his shop trying to perfect his perpetual motion machine. It was pretty creative and impressive, and it would go for a long time; but eventually it would fail.

Everything in life eventually breaks down. Everything will, over time, stop working. But the Bible says that God's love is unfailing. It will never, ever end. It is truly perpetual. It is permanent. It is unceasing. God's love never fails.

Thank God for his unfailing love.

I'm not much of a chess player. I know how to play, but I don't play often. However, I do understand the object of the game. The goal is to get the other person's king while protecting your own. Good chess players set up a strategy that enables them to get their hands on the king.

Most novices try to capture as many of their opponent's men as possible, but that's not the object of the game. You can capture nearly every piece on your opponent's side of the board, but if he slips in and captures your king, the game is over. A good chess player is not focused on gathering his opponent's men. He is focused on capturing the king.

Too many people play at life the way I play chess. They get so focused on accumulating the things of this world that they take their focus off of the king. It doesn't matter how much you accumulate in this world. If you take your eyes off of the king, you've lost!

Don't forget the blessings that God has given you. Don't take your focus off of his blessings! Don't let things like the Thanksgiving killer take your focus off of Jesus.

Next year during Thanksgiving weekend, no, this weekend, and every day in between, don't forget what is most important. Don't let the consumer mentality kill your attitude of thanksgiving.

Stay focused on the king of heaven and be grateful for the blessings he has provided for us. Don't forget about things you have because you are spending too much time thinking about things you want. Thank God for his blessings and receive his blessings. Make them a part of your everyday life.

He offers you forgiveness, availability, protection, instruction, and unfailing love. Take him up on his offer. It is the greatest decision you could ever make.

For Discussion:

1. Have you ever gone shopping early on Black Friday morning? What was it like?
2. How do you think the apostle Paul learned the secret of being content as mentioned in Philippians 4:11-13?
3. Forgiveness can be incredibly liberating. Why is it so hard to do even though we know the rewards of it are great?
4. What have you asked God to protect you from lately?
5. Which one of the five blessings from Psalm 32 are you most thankful for?

2

Another Night
with the Frogs

Procrastination. It's one of our favorite all-time bad habits. There are a lot of things that I like to put off until tomorrow. If I knew I had to go to the dentist and I had a choice of today or tomorrow, I would choose tomorrow. If my wife told me that I needed to go shopping for new clothes at the mall and I had a choice of doing that today or tomorrow, I would choose tomorrow. Every now and then I have to do some repair work around the house. If I had a choice of doing those chores today or tomorrow, I would choose tomorrow.

The truth is that there is a little bit of procrastination in all of us. There are some things we can put off until tomorrow and get away with it. But there are other things we cannot put off until tomorrow. One good thing about procrastination is that you always have something planned for tomorrow.

Have you ever wondered if procrastination is a sin? James 4:17 says, "Anyone, then, who knows the good he ought to do and doesn't do it, sins."

Wow! That's pretty strong. Does that mean because we didn't paint our bedroom over the Christmas holidays like we said we were going to do, we sinned against God? Does that mean because I haven't cleaned out the gutters yet that I am sinning? No, I don't think James is talking about that kind of procrastination. But I do think he means that anything we know we should do, as it relates to our relationship with God and others, and we don't do it, it's a sin.

Procrastination is really nothing more than being irresponsible, lazy, and self-centered. In some cases, like painting the bedroom or cleaning out the gutters, it's not a big deal. But if our procrastination has a negative effect on our relationship with God or others, then it is wrong.

When we put off things that we cannot put off until tomorrow, we run into big problems. In Exodus 8, Pharaoh did that and he ran into big problems.

At the end of the book of Genesis, Joseph's family had gone into Egypt because of famine. He found favor with the Pharoah and became a high ranking official in Egypt. Joseph died and as the years passed, the new Pharaoh forgot about Joseph and his family. The new Pharaoh enslaved the Israelites. God sent Moses to the Pharaoh to represent Israel.

Moses demanded that Pharaoh release the Israelites so that they could worship God freely. If Pharaoh refused, God sent plagues on Egypt. There were a total of ten. Pharaoh was hardheaded and hardhearted. He refused the first time, so God sent a plague of blood on the land of Egypt. All water was turned to blood - the water of the Nile River, its tributaries, ponds, even the water in buckets.

The Lord told Moses to go back to Pharaoh and implore him to let Israel go or else the land would be plagued with frogs. Frogs would be everywhere - in the Pharaoh's palace, even his bedroom, and in the people's homes including their ovens!

God could have plagued Egypt with lions or bears or wolves or snakes or vultures, but he chose to do it with some of his smallest creatures. You know, for most people, one or two frogs are cute and fun to watch. But thousands and thousands of frogs are disgusting. In the plagues that followed, God sent gnats, flies, and locusts. I've always thought that cockroaches would have been a good plague. Isn't it funny how God used the smallest pests of creation against Pharaoh? Don't you know it humbled Pharaoh to be defeated by some of the smallest, less intimidating, creations of God?

But why frogs? Why did God send a plague of frogs, and why didn't the Egyptians just kill the frogs? They couldn't. The Egyptian goddess of Heqet was the goddess of fertility. She was depicted in the form of a woman with a frog's head.

I dated a girl in high school that looked like Heqet.

The Egyptians believed that Heqet blew the breath of life into the nostrils of all living beings. To them, the frog was a sacred animal representing fertility. They could not kill it. It was like God was giving them a dose of their own medicine. They didn't want any part of God. They were satisfied with their own way of living and with the gods that they had created, and God was letting them be more than satisfied with it. He was letting them be consumed by their god.

> Pharaoh summoned Moses and Aaron and said, "Pray to the Lord to take the frogs away from me and my people, and I will let your people go to offer sacrifices to the Lord." Moses said to Pharaoh, "I leave to you the honor of setting the time for me to pray for you and your officials and your people that you and your houses may be rid of the frogs, except for those that remain in the Nile." "Tomorrow," Pharaoh said. (Exodus 8:8-10)

Pharaoh was willing to spend another night with the frogs. Why would he choose to wait until the next day? Is the power of procrastination that strong? Is apathy that strong? Perhaps he had his servants clean out his room in the palace. Maybe the frogs weren't as large of a burden to him and, therefore, he didn't care. Maybe Pharaoh had strategically posted guards around him with the exclusive assignment of shooing the frogs away from his presence. Maybe he liked fried frog legs, and he was enjoying the recent bounty of his unusual delicacy. For whatever reason, Pharaoh was content to live another day with a plague of frogs. The Egyptians were plagued with frogs.

What frogs are plaguing you?

Are they the same things that plagued you this time last year? Did you decide over the last 365 nights that you could stand one more night with those frogs? And did one more night become another night and then another night and then a week and then a month until you've gone another year with the frogs? Do you want to go through this month with the same frogs plaguing you? Are you going to spend another night with the frogs?

What are the frogs that are plaguing your life? Dealing with a shaky marriage? Are you just putting band aids on your problems instead of doing what you know to do to make your marriage great? Is debt plaguing you? What about your weight or health? Is your job plaguing you? Completing your education? An addiction problem? Relationships? Lack of spiritual devotion? Salvation? What are you putting off until tomorrow that should have been done a long time ago? How can this old story in Exodus relate to your tendency to procrastinate today?

Listen Today

When God speaks today, don't put off listening until tomorrow. To put off listening to God is to ask for trouble. Pharaoh did not want to hear from God that day because he had plans for the Israelite slave labor to keep building his buildings. This was not a good time for God to be talking to Pharaoh. I'm sure Pharaoh was thinking, "Can you come back and talk to me about this another time? I'm in the middle of a huge construction project."

We do the same thing. We put God off.

"God, this is not a good time right now. I am so busy raising my children. After they are grown up, I will have more time for you."

"God, it is not a good time because I am working hard for that promotion. After I get that promotion, I will have more time to listen to you."

"God, I don't have time to serve you right now, but when things slow down a little, I'll see what I can do."

What are you doing today to hear from God? What are you doing today to grow closer to God? We know that God charges us to grow spiritually and to serve, but we put him off until tomorrow. Are you reading? Are you studying? Are you praying and meditating on God's Word? Are you engaged with other believers in a small group? Are you utilizing your gifts and talents for ministry?

Are you doing more than just showing up for church on Sundays? Are you a spectator or a participant? Peter wrote, "Grow in the grace and knowledge of our Lord and Savior Jesus Christ."[2] You need to grow up in the faith. This is not written as a suggestion, but a command.

Are you listening to God today? Don't put it off another day.

Obey Today

> At midnight the Lord struck down all the firstborn in Egypt, from the firstborn of Pharaoh, who sat on the throne, to the firstborn of the prisoner, who was in the dungeon, and the firstborn of all the livestock as well. Pharaoh and all his officials and all the Egyptians got up during the night, and there was loud wailing in Egypt, for there was not a house without someone dead. (Exodus 12:29-30)

When God requires my obedience today, I cannot give it to him tomorrow without experiencing the consequences today.

Pharaoh didn't obey God, and he suffered the consequences. We see elsewhere in the Bible that delayed obedience brings problems, e.g., Jonah refused to go to Ninevah, and he ended up spending three days as fish food. We do this all of the time. You know that God has called you to do something but you put it off until tomorrow, and it makes your today worse - and it makes tomorrow worse too!

What about the plague of debt? Every day with credit card debt earns more money for the bank and creates more money you have to pay back. It happens slowly but, in the end, will cost you hundreds or thousands of dollars.

If you're struggling with an addiction, every additional day with that addiction drives it deeper into your life. Like driving a nail into a piece of wood, each time you acknowledge your craving, the addiction goes in further and becomes harder and harder to remove. Waiting until tomorrow to remove it only makes it harder to overcome today.

Addictions are like a cancer. If ignored, they will grow and fester and soon take over your life. But, once acknowledged and treated, they can be contained and ultimately defeated if you attack them in due time. If you maintain the disciplines required making today successful, your tomorrows will not be a nightmare, and you will take care of one of the frogs that may be plaguing you today.

Consider Others Today

I should not put off until tomorrow anything that as a result of my procrastination will create hardship for someone else today.

Pharaoh's refusal to listen to God caused problems for his entire kingdom. We call that stubbornness, selfishness, meanness, or being hard-headed. Pharaoh not only made this a battle between him and God, but he involved the whole nation in the battle. When it came to his reluctance to give in to God, he involved everyone.

Out of stubbornness and hardheadedness, we are going to hurt people. Is one of the frogs in your life a bad habit or an addiction that will create a hardship for a loved one? You may be a chronic speeder, i.e., taking a risk every time you get on the highway. You may be a smoker shortening your life with every drag of a cigarette. You may be a glutton causing your heart to pump even harder because you're not watching your intake.

When you do these things, you're not only risking your life, but you're putting your loved ones in a precarious position. They may be planning your funeral sooner than expected and having to make ends meet without you soon. Your hardheadedness will become a hardship for others.

Or maybe your situation is not so morbid. Maybe your lack of planning causes hardship for your coworkers or employees. Maybe your lack of compassion causes friction in some relationships. Maybe your chronic tardiness prevents work from getting done and wastes other people's time. Maybe your neglect with certain responsibilities creates more work for others. Maybe your inability to humble yourself brings tension and makes issues more difficult than they ought to be. It can be a number of things.

If your procrastination has negative consequences for others, you need to examine those things. Don't put them off until tomorrow.

Pray Today

If I don't know how to talk to God today, I may not be able to talk to God when I need him tomorrow.

Pharaoh asked Moses and Aaron to pray that God would take the frogs away from him. Pharaoh couldn't talk to the Lord because he had no experience. Moses had to talk to God for Pharaoh.[3]

Are you able to talk to God on your own? It's just a matter of having a conversation with a dear friend. Be honest with him. Be open and genuine. God already knows your heart. Don't be afraid to reveal it. Ask him the hard questions. Tell him when you're struggling. Beg for his mercy. Whatever you need to let him know, say it.

When I speak to people who struggle with their prayer life, I often encourage them to write out their prayers. Writing a letter to God requires more concentration and thought. You're not as easily distracted when you're writing. The cool thing about writing your prayers is that you can keep them and read them later to see how God answered those prayers. I have many spiral notebooks with my prayers and thoughts from years ago. Every once in a while, I'll pull them out and skim through them. It's a great way to store the history of my spiritual life as well as affirmation that God does indeed answer my prayers.

If you don't make it a habit to pray now, when will you pray? When you get in a desperate situation? Is that the only time you're going to pray? When you have a crucial need? Then maybe you don't understand prayer. Prayer isn't just petitioning God with all of our needs and wants. Prayer is communing with our Heavenly Father. It's focusing on him, not our needs. Prayer is not reaching for things in the hand of God. It's reaching *for* the hand of God.

If you're not praying today, will you know how to pray tomorrow? Don't put off prayer for another time or a more crucial need. Learn to pray today. Speak to God everyday, all day, just as you would speak with your best friend if he were right beside you.

If you learn how to pray today, your tomorrows will be blessed.

Don't Go Alone Today

Sometimes I wait until tomorrow with God because I want to see if I can do it without him today.

Why would Pharaoh wait until tomorrow to get rid of the frogs? Because he wanted time to do everything humanly possible to get rid of the frogs without calling on God. He bought time to see if his magicians could get rid of them. He bought time to see if the frogs would die on their own.

We wait until we are in the bottom of the pit to call on God. We wait until our backs are against the wall before we cry out to God. We wait until we are completely miserable before we beg for his mercy. We want to try it on our own. We want to leave God out. We are stubborn enough to say, "I don't need God in this situation. I can get out of this mess myself."

Someone said, "Procrastination is like fertilizer. It helps difficulties grow." When we try to solve our own problems instead of taking them to God, one of two things typically happens:

1. The problems get worse instead of better.
2. The problem is solved, but it took longer or was more difficult because we left God out of the equation.

Working independently of God is nothing more than a complete lack of faith. Deciding to wait on God and solve our own problems without him is a slap in God's face. You may as well say, "God, I don't need you. You are of no value to me."

Suppose you wanted to learn how to pilot an airplane. How ridiculous would it be for you to arrive at the airport for your first lesson and climb directly into the pilot's seat in an airplane and try to fly that plane without any help? Would you think to yourself, "I'll see how far I can get in this plane on my own first. If I need help, I'll ask for it when I get desperate."

Why do we do that with God? He created us. He created everything around us. He knows our current situation and our future. Why not trust him today instead of waiting until things get worse tomorrow? Don't try to get rid of your frogs on your own. Get God involved in your life today, and ask him to take care of the things that are plaguing you.

Fulfill your Promises Today

When my prayers move God to action today, I had better not put off until tomorrow what I had promised him.

Pharaoh promised God he would let Moses' people go if God would remove the frogs. God acted based on that promise, and then Pharaoh never followed through. Once the frogs were gone, Pharaoh hardened his heart and decided to continue holding the nation of Israel hostage.

We don't ever do that, do we? The truth is that we often make promises to God, but we don't follow through. "Oh, God! If you'll just help me with this problem, I promise I'll be a better servant!" "Oh, God! If you'll just get me through this situation, I'll be the Christian you want me to be!"

What promises do you owe God that you have not followed through on? Have you ever promised to give God your life and not followed up on it? Have you ever promised God that you would be a fully devoted follower? Do you refuse to submit your life to God because you'd rather do it on your own? Do you know your need for him, but you're too stubborn to hand the keys of your life to God? You know he's a better pilot, but you like having control. What are you waiting on? A deathbed repentance? That's a big risk you're taking. Are you sowing your wild oats now, and are you going to get serious about God when you get older? Who says you're going to get older? The Bible says not to boast about tomorrow. You don't know if you're going to be here tomorrow. Life is like a mist that's here for a little while, then it vanishes.⁴ When are you going to give your life totally to Christ?

Are you trying to clean up your life first, and then give it to God? You've got it backwards. Let Jesus into your dirty life and he will come in and clean it up. You can't clean up the sin in your life - that's something only Jesus can do. What are you waiting for? Why are you not asking God to be in charge of every part of your life? Do you really, sincerely believe that you can manage your life better than the one who created you? That's as absurd as me telling Bill Gates to move over so that I can run Microsoft!

Do you really want to spend another night with the frogs? Do you really want to spend another year with the same things plaguing you night after night? Give it to God. He will transform your life completely. Don't ignore him any longer. Whether it's the decision to let him be your Lord and Savior for the very first time or whether you are a veteran Christian with a few problems that you're hiding – let God in today, not tomorrow, and he will give you the grace to accomplish incredible tasks if you let him.

For Discussion:

1. What's on your "things-to-do list" that hasn't been done yet?

2. What are you putting off until tomorrow that should have been done a long time ago?

3. Why do we tend to go to God for help as a last resort?

4. Can you recall a time when you were the victim of someone's procrastination? How did that affect your relationship with that person?

5. "Working independent of God is nothing more than a complete lack of faith." Do you believe that is true? Why?

3

The Joy of Do-Overs

When I was a kid, my yard was a multisports arena. We played baseball, football, basketball, and golf. We had bicycle jumps, zip lines off the roof of the house, and historic pinecone fights. Great memories were made playing games in my yard.

But our stadium wasn't perfect. Sometimes the game was interrupted by tree limbs, power lines, dogs, or cars coming down the road. Sometimes a potential touchdown pass would hit a limb or sometimes a ground ball would roll out into the street and hit a passing car. Occasionally, in the middle of a drive to the goal for a lay up, the neighbor's dog would run through the defense and trip up a player.

In cases like these, when the game was interrupted we had what we called a "do-over." Any kid that has played sandlot baseball knows about do-overs. A do-over is called when something unexpected or unforeseen takes place in a game, and the teams aren't sure how to rule it; so you do it again.

Sometimes we knew the potential before a game began, and we would make it a rule before we started. If the ball goes on the roof, you can catch it off the roof. If the ball arrives at the base at the exact same time as the runner, a tie goes to the runner. If the ball goes out in the street, it's a ground rule double. If a golf ball hits a car, everybody runs as fast as possible.

I was at a South Carolina Gamecocks football game a few years ago when a punt hit the wire that held a television camera hovering above the field. They called for a do-over. I've never seen that happen in an official game like that. In golf, a do-over is called a mulligan. If you don't like your shot, you take another one, but usually only one per round.

There is a toy that teaches us about the joy of do-overs - the Etch-A-Sketch - the classic do-over toy. You probably had an Etch-A-Sketch in your home at some time in your life. With an Etch-A-Sketch, you can create all kinds of weird designs and drawings. The possibilities are endless. The great thing is, if you mess up, you simply turn it over and shake it, and you have a clean slate.

Have you noticed that we live in an "Etch-A-Sketch" culture now? Everybody wants a do-over. The TV industry has gone berserk with makeover shows. Women undergo plastic surgery and public humiliation on TV in a supposed effort to feel better about themselves. The result is that they all look pretty much the same at the end of the day: long, swingy hair (usually blonde), improved figure, slinky gowns, very Vegas, and very predictable. At the end of the makeover, regardless of each woman's wants, needs, hopes, dreams, they're all made into the same creature. They all look alike. Apparently they think that you can inject self-confidence with a syringe, but it is not so.

HGTV alone has 22 makeover shows. There is another one called *What Not to Wear,* and, of course, let's not forget *Queer Eye for the Straight Guy.*

Hollywood loves this idea. My favorite Christmas movie of all time, *It's a Wonderful Life,* gives George Bailey (played by Jimmy Stewart) a chance to see what life would be like without him. He gets a new outlook on life after his experience.

Groundhog Day with Bill Murray featured a news reporter who was able to change his approach to life on Groundhog Day until he got it right. In *Clean Slate,* Dana Carvey plays a private detective who forgets everything when he goes to sleep at night and wakes up each morning with a "clean slate." Adam Sandler plays a veterinarian who falls in love with a woman with short-term memory loss in *50 First Dates.* Each time they meet, he has to find a way to get her to fall in love with him all over again. You can probably think of other films with similar storylines.

In a way, all of us are looking for a do-over. No one wants to face up to his imperfections. No one wants to remember her boo-boos, and no one wants to bring up her past mistakes.

At times, everyone wants a chance to start over. Why? Sometimes we make poor choices, and we'd like to make up for them. Sometimes our bad decisions hold us back. Sometimes our mistakes interfere with our future plans.

This is one reason why people change jobs. It's a chance to start over. But we can't turn back time, can we? New Year's Day is the closest we come. There is something about beginning a new year that gives us the feeling of new life. Something about January 1 gives us hope for the future and the ability to shut the door on the past. If there were ever a day for do-overs and clean slates, it is January 1. For me, the beginning of the school year is a time for new beginnings. Since my wife is a school teacher, mid-August always begins a new routine that lasts until early June. August is also a time of evaluation and introspection. I often get a fresh start in the fall.

Whether it's a new calendar year or a new school year, these seasons cause us to think about time and our use or abuse of it. Time is the one thing in our lives that cannot be replaced or made up. You could lose one million dollars and make it back later. It has been done before. But if you lose one million minutes, you can never use that time again.

The Greek god of time was named Kronos. He had long hair hanging in front of his face, so he could be grasped from the front. But the back of his head was bald, so that no one could take hold of him once he had raced by.

President Ronald Reagan noticed that the pilots who flew Air Force One touched down as close to the beginning of the runway as possible. One day he asked one of the pilots why. The pilot answered, "Sir, one of the first things pilots learn is that you can't use the runway behind you."

You may not be able to capture lost time but God has provided a way for you to start over. "Therefore, if anyone is in Christ, he is a new creation; the old has gone, the new has come!"[5]

What this means is that those who become Christ-followers become new people. They are not the same anymore. The old life is gone. A new life has begun. Jesus called it being born again. It is a complete change. It gives a new outlook and perspective on life. Becoming a new creation renews your mind.

The apostle Paul wrote to the Philippian church that being a new creation in Christ was his primary focus.

I don't mean to say that I have already achieved these things or that I have already reached perfection! But I keep working toward that day when I will finally be all that Christ Jesus saved me for and wants me to be. No, dear brothers and sisters, I am still not all I should be, but I am focusing all my energies on this one thing: Forgetting the past and looking forward to what lies ahead, I strain to reach the end of the race and receive the prize for which God, through Christ Jesus, is calling us up to heaven. (Philippians 3:12-14, NLT)

How can you start over, and how can you reach the prize of God? How can I get a do-over?

Listen to the Ultimate Authority

Three people today need no last names: Dr. Phil, Oprah, and Dr. Laura. We've all heard of them. Dr. Phil McGraw, the Texas psychologist, was made famous by Oprah Winfrey, now has his own television show seen by five million people daily and three best-selling books. Dr. Laura Schlessinger, the radio counselor and therapist heard across the nation, is also the author of numerous best-selling books. Of course, Oprah is the most amazing media phenomenon of our time. Most Americans would do nearly anything to get personal advice from these three celebrity experts.

With no disrespect to these media therapists, there is one more experienced than Dr. Phil, one more wise than Dr. Laura, and even one more powerful than Oprah. The one who said, "All authority in heaven and on earth has been given to me."[6]

His name is Jesus. He is the ultimate authority in everything. Look at that verse closely. "All" means every kind of, over every sphere and area of life. "Authority" means power, control, ownership, direction. "In heaven and on earth" means in every realm of the universe. No king, dictator, general, president, czar, media giant, or any other human being has ever made such a claim. Jesus shares this authority with no other person. It has been given to him and him alone.

Dr. Phil doesn't know your name, but Jesus does. Dr. Laura can't see your future, but Jesus can. Oprah cannot meet all your needs, but Jesus will. It makes sense to me that I should listen to the one who wants what is best for me, and, - oh, by the way - he also happens to have complete and ultimate authority over creation. Don't you think you should investigate Jesus' advice for your life?

Jesus is about change. He can come into your life and give you an extreme makeover. I know because he did it for me, and I have seen him do it for thousands of other people. You need to decide to listen to the one who has ultimate authority.

Start with New Birth

The decision to change is most important. You need to recognize that you can't be successful in life by yourself. You need help. You need to recognize that you cannot receive the prize that God has for you on your own. You need to recognize that you can't earn your own way.

Nothing you can do is good enough. The prophet Isaiah wrote, "All of us have become like one who is unclean, and all our righteous acts are like filthy rags; we all shrivel up like a leaf, and like the wind our sins sweep us away."[7]

Even on our best day, we have sin in our lives. Jesus said that, in order to get a new start, one must be born again. That starts with recognizing that we cannot do that on our own. We must take care of the filthy rags in our life. We must admit that we have sinned, and that, in order to have the holy God in our life, we must confess our sin to him.

Paul, the apostle, had the right family heritage. He was the result of some of the highest education available. He was properly trained as a Jewish leader. Look at his claim in his letter to the Philippians.

> If anyone else thinks he has reasons to put confidence in the flesh, I have more: circumcised on the eighth day, of the people of Israel, of the tribe of Benjamin, a Hebrew of Hebrews; in regard to the law, a Pharisee; as for zeal, persecuting the church; as for legalistic righteousness, faultless. But whatever was to my profit I now consider loss for the sake of Christ. What is more, I consider everything a loss compared to the surpassing greatness of knowing Christ Jesus my Lord, for whose sake I have lost all things. I consider them rubbish that I may gain Christ. (Philippians 3:4-8)

Paul realized that even with his impressive resume, he was doomed without Christ. He realized that, without Christ, he was a loser. Everything he had accomplished and accumulated was nothing but garbage compared to Christ.

If you want a do-over, you have to allow Christ to be central to your life.

Take Care of Your Past

I am still not all I should be, but I am focusing all my energies on this one thing: Forgetting the past and looking forward to what lies ahead. (Philippians 3:13, NLT)

In order to take care of the sins of our past, sometimes we have to seek restitution. We have to take bold steps to repair relationships that we dirtied with our filthy rags.

A friend of mine became a Christ-follower during his high school years and even felt a call to the ministry when he was a teenager. He went to college on an athletic scholarship with a strong reputation as a follower of Christ. But it didn't take too long for the college party scene to knock on his door and he answered. He turned to the party life and said goodbye to his faith. After a year or two of radical narcissistic living, he finally got a wake-up call and came back to Christ and reconciled his relationship with him.

But he had done some damage and he needed to do damage control. He tarnished his reputation as a Christ-follower. Convicted about the poor choices he had made in the past, he went personally to everyone possible (mostly teammates) to confess his filthy rags and ask for their forgiveness. For those who were no longer on the campus or in the area where he lived, he wrote letters or made phone calls asking for forgiveness.

In order to put the past behind you, sometimes you have to come clean - that may mean repairing and rebuilding broken relationships. Maybe you need to sit down and write a few letters or make a few phone calls. It may mean paying back money that you owe. It may mean repairing someone's personal property that you damaged. Anything God tells you to take care of to forget the past, take care of it. Once those things are taken care of, put them behind you, and look toward nothing but your future.

God has a ministry plan for you, no matter your past mistakes, present circumstances, or future fears. John Bunyan spent twelve years in jail, imprisoned for preaching the gospel. Did this end his ministry? No, it was in prison where he wrote *The Pilgrim's Progress*, the most influential Christian book of all time, next to the Bible. Charles Colson was embarrassed as he was sentenced to federal prison in the Watergate scandal; yet, he turned what could have been a life-ending and career-ending event into a positive and started an international ministry called Prison Fellowship. Colson is now one of the great authors and spokesmen for Christianity in this generation.

God can take a bankrupt life and make it rich. He can turn failures into overwhelming victories. He can turn disasters into blessings.

Thomas Edison contributed much to society, the incandescent light bulb, the phonograph, and he improved the telephone with a carbon transmitter that meant users did not need to shout. He had many successes. But one night his laboratory caught fire, and he could only watch his life's work as it burned to ashes. In fact, during the fire he told his son to go get his mother. "She'll never see anything like this as long as she lives." The day after his lab burned, Thomas Edison said, "There is great value in disaster. All our mistakes are burned up. Thank God we can start anew."

God will give you all the power and help you need to accomplish his ministry purpose for your life. A. W. Tozer was right: "God is looking for those through whom he can do the impossible - what a pity that we plan only the things that we can do by ourselves." Paul wrote, "I can do everything through him who gives me strength."[8]

Be a Disciple of Christ

Paul wrote to the church in Philippi, "But I keep working toward that day when I will finally be all that Christ Jesus saved me for and wants me to be."[9]

Let your future dwell on being a disciple of Christ. Let your future be working toward being all that Christ saved you for and wants you to be. One of Jesus' last commands was, "Go and make disciples of all nations."[10] Making disciples was Jesus' central purpose and task. The word "disciple" appears in the Gospels 230 times. Jesus prayed all night before selecting his first disciples.[11] He lived with them for three years. He entrusted his mission into their hands. His first priority was making disciples. It is our priority as well.

But what is a disciple? In the ancient world, a "disciple" was an apprentice, someone who enrolled in a school or learned from a teacher in a personal relationship. The Jewish rabbis had their disciples, students who chose them and were taught the Law by them.

Unlike the rabbis, Jesus chose his students.[12] He called them to leave everything to follow him. He taught them to teach others. A disciple of Jesus was a person who followed him with full commitment and devotion and led others to do the same. They were reproducing imitators of Jesus.

Jesus commanded that we are to go into the entire world. We are not to wait for the world to find us, but we are to go to the world. We are designed to make an impact on people not just in our community but in all nations. I sincerely believe that every believer should take this command seriously. It is God's purpose for us to be and build disciples of Christ.

Why is being a disciple and making disciples God's purpose? There are two reasons. First: Disciple making is the key to reaching the nations with his love. If I lead one person to Christ every day for 33 years, 12,045 people would be in heaven. But if I lead one person a year and disciple him so that he can reproduce himself by leading another, and this process continues at the rate of one per year for 33 years, 8,589,934,592 people would be in heaven, more than the entire population of the world.

Second: Disciple making is the only purpose for which God made us. It is the only purpose that gives our lives meaning, satisfaction, and significance. There's been a lot of talk about purpose in the last few years. Rick Warren's book, *The Purpose Driven Life*, has caused many to think about their purpose in life. Warren was able to narrow life's purpose down to five things: worship, service, evangelism, fellowship, and discipleship. But really those five disciplines are the disciplines of a disciple of Christ. If you are a disciple of Christ, you'll put these five disciplines (or purposes) in your life.

One of the most significant trends of our day is called "baby boomer hasbeenhood." (Maybe you've seen t-shirts that say "The older I get, the better I was"). Seventy-six million Americans are considered baby-boomers (i.e., those born between 1946 and 1964). A cottage industry has formed to help them find a new purpose for their lives. Firms exist to help aging executives transition. There is a popular book by Bob Buford called *Finishing Well* that talks about how to successfully live the second half of your life. Thousands of career counselors stay busy helping members of this generation find the next stage in their careers and new meaning for their lives.

But unfortunately for some, it's not working. Alcohol purchases in America are up 20% in three years. One in five boomers will suffer from depression, one of the most debilitating diseases of our time. Nearly twice as many Americans die from the tragedy of suicide as from homicide.

I can appreciate the wisdom of Abraham Maslow's words: "An artist must paint, a poet must write, a musician must make music if he is to be ultimately at peace with himself." To be at peace with yourself, you must fulfill the purpose for which you were created and that purpose is to be and make disciples of Christ.

We need to make Christ our number one priority in life.

The summer after my high school graduation, my parents and I spent a week in Cairo, Egypt. While there, we visited the Egyptian National Museum. The King Tut exhibit was mind-boggling. King Tut was only 17 when he died. He was buried with solid gold chariots and thousands of gold artifacts. His gold coffin was found within gold tombs within gold tombs within gold tombs. The burial site was filled with gold.

The Egyptians believed that they could take earthly treasures with them, but all of the treasures intended for King Tut's afterlife were still in his grave until they were discovered in 1922 - over 3000 years later.

Not far from the museum, if you go down the dusty streets of Cairo and turn down an alley, you will find a plot of overgrown grass. It is a graveyard for American missionaries. At the top of one old tombstone it says, "William Borden, 1887-1913." Borden was twenty-five years old when he died.

William Borden graduated from both Yale and Princeton and was a multi-millionaire due to his family's business, i.e., Borden Dairies. In many ways he was the King Tut of his day. William Borden could have lived a life of luxury but instead chose to give his life as a disciple of Christ. He had a burden to be a disciple maker as a missionary to the Muslim world. He refused to spend money on himself and instead gave hundreds of thousands of dollars to the ministry. He died when he contracted spinal meningitis at the age of 25 while serving in Egypt.

If you dust off his tombstone further, you will read on his epitaph his love for God and the Muslim people. The inscription ends with this phrase, "Apart from faith in Christ, there is no explanation for such a life."

What a contrast! One man was buried with a ridiculous amount of gold and the other was buried in an obscure, dusty, overgrown, back alley graveyard. One lived in complete opulence with everything the world had to offer, and the other lived a modest life of service to the one true King. William Borden is enjoying his everlasting reward in the presence of God today.

King Tut's life was tragic because of an awful truth discovered too late – you can't take it with you. William Borden's life was triumphant because instead of leaving his treasures behind, he sent them ahead.

"Apart from faith in Christ, there is no explanation for such a life." I wonder if this can be said of your life? If not, you can get a do-over. Will you determine to be a disciple of Christ? You can become a new creation in Christ. You can put away the things of the past and press on in your future with Christ. What will it take for you to be all that Christ Jesus saved you for and wants you to be?

For Discussion

1. What event(s) in your life would you like to do over?
2. Read 2 Corinthians 5:17. Does this verse apply to your life? If not, what are you waiting on?
3. Why do people gravitate toward the advice of the latest, greatest pop psychologists when God's wisdom is clearly given to us in the Bible?
4. Talk about someone you may know who was able to leave their jaded past behind them and start a new life in Christ. How did that person deal with their past?
5. Read Matthew 28:18-20. If our mission and purpose in life is to make disciples, why does this task seem to be unnatural for us?

4

God Chooses You

There were many ways to choose teams before a ball game began in my multi-sport arena backyard. The method to select teammates was often the game before the game. We could do the potato method, (i.e., one potato, two potato, three potato, four...). Last potato standing won. We could pick a number behind a random person's back. The person with the most accurate guess would begin picking his team first. Before a baseball game, we would do the bat climb. Two captains would work their hands up the barrel of the bat. The one whose hand covered the top of the bat was the winner.

If two guys happened to be bigger and older, they typically made themselves team captains. The more superior of the two would often say something like, "I'll take these two and you can have the rest." Two lop-sided teams would take the field, but the talent would be somewhat equally distributed.

Whatever method was chosen, there was always some sort of line-up involved. After captains and first pick was determined, the rest of the players would line up to be selected by the team captain. The best athletes were chosen first, of course. The rest of us would stand at attention, poke our chests out, and try to impress the selectors so that we wouldn't be the last ones chosen.

I was usually one of the youngest and smallest in the bunch and, as a result, I was often the last one chosen. That's what happens when you pick teams like that. The biggest and the best are always picked first. Maybe you've experienced the embarrassment of being picked last. You were considered the least athletic, the least popular, or the runt of the litter. You hoped that just once you wouldn't be picked last, but every time it was the same - last. "Okay," the final chooser would say with resignation in his voice. "We'll take Gene."

In Paul's letter to the Corinthians he asks them to survey their own congregation.[13] Apparently, this group of believers had a short supply of people who were wise scholars or experts. There were few influential people in the church and not many who were socially elite. If God chose people based on human criteria, the group in Corinth would have been passed by. Humans like people with brains, clout, and pedigrees. But God isn't like us. The kid who is always picked last on the playground is often the one God picks first.

From Foolish to Wise

Most of us are just average folk. When God called you to be part of his family, you might have thought, "Why me? I'm a nobody."

God specializes in taking nobodies and making them somebody. He did it with me. When I think of what I was like before I discovered Christ, it's a little embarrassing. I was aimless, without purpose, trying to make an impression, definitely not in the academic circles, nor was I in the influential group, and positively not born in the high-society crowd. But God chose a fool like me to represent him. He welcomed a foolish and pimply 17-year-old into his family, and it was the greatest thing that will ever happen to me.

Paul wrote that God chose the foolish things to shame the wise.[14] The word Paul used for "foolish" is the Greek word "mora." We get the word "moron" from this word. It means to be dull or stupid. Isn't that encouraging? Don't you know the Corinthians liked hearing Paul call them morons?

The story is told of an agnostic anthropologist who visited some islands in the South Pacific. He was critical of the chief of the tribe. "You're a great leader, but it's a pity you've been taken in by those Christian missionaries. They only want to get rich through you. No one believes the Bible anymore. People are tired of the story of Christ dying on a cross for the sins of mankind. They know better now. It's foolish for you to accept their story."

The old chief said, "Do you see that big rock over there? That's where we used to smash the heads of our victims. See the furnace next to it? That's where we used to roast the bodies of our enemies. If it hadn't been for those good missionaries and the love of Jesus that changed us from cannibals into Christians, we'd be eating you for supper tonight. You'd better be glad I'm a fool for Christ."

What appears to be foolish in the eyes of man is wise in the eyes of God.

Why Did God Choose Fools?

It never ceases to amaze me to see the people that God chooses to do his work. We would choose the wise, the mighty, and the elite. Instead, God uses ordinary people. We often think that God cannot use us. We have no talents that God can use. We have no gifts. We have no ability. We have no education. We have no experience. We have no strength. We have no "know-how." We have no opportunity. We have no confidence in ourselves.

God chooses ordinary people to do his work. He equips and gifts his people with the ability to serve him. God doesn't need your ability. He will give you abilities. What God wants is your availability.

Consider the choosing of King David.[15] Saul had been rejected as king, and God sent Samuel to anoint a new king. Jesse, David's dad, had his sons line up so that Samuel could see Jesse's lot. Surely the oldest son, Eliab, would be chosen but Samuel passed on him. Surely the second son, Abinadab, would be chosen but Samuel overlooked him too. Maybe Samuel would choose the third son, Shammah, but Samuel did not choose him either. All seven of Jesse's sons were rejected.

Samuel asked, "Are these all your children?" There was one more, the youngest son, David, the shepherd boy. The one that was not even considered worthy to be called to the line up was chosen by God. David became Israel's greatest king ever. God used David to establish his kingdom, to gather the materials to build the Temple, and to write most of the Psalms.

There was a man born nearly 300 years ago. He was eleven years old when he began working on ships in the Mediterranean Sea. He once tried to run away, and he was demoted to the lowest rank on the ship. He had a reputation as being one of the most undisciplined, rude, and foul-mouthed sailors. He was so bad that few captains wanted him on their vessel. Eventually, he was given his own ship - a slave ship. He would take slaves by the hundreds to the new world until one night he was caught in a storm, and it seemed that the ship would sink, and all would be lost. On May 10, 1748, he gave his life to Jesus Christ. He soon quit as the captain of the slave ship. He would go on to study for the ministry, and God used John Newton to write one of the greatest hymns in all of Christianity. "Amazing Grace, how sweet the sound that saved a wretch like me. I once was lost but now am found 'twas blind but now I see."

If God can use a shepherd boy and turn him into a king and if God can make a songwriter out of a slave trader, he can use you.

Blow a Trumpet for God

"It is because of him that you are in Christ Jesus."[16] God chose you not for who you are but for who he is. God loves all men regardless of their achievements, position, or family heritage. He has chosen you based on what he can do through you, not what you can do for him.

For all those who have answered God's call in Jesus Christ, he has granted us wisdom, righteousness, holiness, and freedom.[17] This is what we should boast about. Not anything we've done, but what Christ has done for us!

> Everything that we have - right thinking and right living, a clean slate and a fresh start - comes from God by way of Jesus Christ. That's why we have the saying, "If you're going to blow a horn, blow a trumpet for God." (1 Corinthians 1:30-31, MSG)

Maybe this is how "Honk If You Love Jesus" bumper stickers started?

God Works through Our Disabilities

I do not have great eloquence or superior wisdom. I can tell you that many times there is weakness, fear, and trembling. I'll never forget my first real experience as a preacher. My first official appearance as a professional pulpiteer was in Los Angeles, California. I was a South Carolina boy from a Texas seminary in La-La land as a revival preacher/evangelist scheduled to speak at a week-long revival meeting. Nine services in a row, Sunday morning, Sunday night, and every night through the next Sunday morning.

For some reason, I thought I needed a different suit for each service. I didn't own any luggage, so I arrived from Dallas/Ft. Worth airport at LAX with my wife's matching pink luggage including pink hanging bag with nine suits. I was confident enough in my masculinity to carry pink suitcases through LA, but my confidence in my evangelistic skills were cause for concern. I was anxious before my first appearance that Sunday morning and worried about blending with the California culture with a Southern accent. Ten minutes before the service began, I overheard a senior adult lady say to a friend, "I'm glad this year's preacher is from Texas. The fellow we had last year was from South Carolina, and I couldn't understand a word he said."

Enter nausea.

Believe it or not, God used this pitiful excuse for a revivalist that week. God spoke to some people and lives were reinvigorated - at least temporarily. It was definitely not because of my great eloquence or superior wisdom. It was totally because of God working through a rookie preacher from the Deep South.

The truth is, I've heard a lot of popular speakers who are not the most eloquent, entertaining, or scholarly presenters. But God uses them because they are usable. That is what God wants, availability. You let him have your abilities, no matter how feeble they might be, and make yourself available, and he will use your humble service to draw others close to him.

Believe it or not, Paul was not an outstanding orator. He mentioned in one of his letters to the church in Corinth that some say, "His letters are weighty and forceful, but in person he is unimpressive and his speaking amounts to nothing."[18]

Paul writes that he did not intend to preach "with wise and persuasive words but with a demonstration of the Spirit's power, so that your faith might not rest on men's wisdom, but on God's power."[19] He did not want to speak in such a way that his human effort would persuade people. He depended on God's Holy Spirit and divine power to do the work.

What does this mean for us in our everyday lives? You should live obediently for Christ, loving him, worshipping him, serving him, and trusting him. You should live out your faith within your own unique personality in the places where God has placed you with the people that God has put around you and depend on his Holy Spirit to speak through your life with wisdom and power.

You do what you know you should do, and God will take care of the rest. You will be amazed at what God can do through ordinary you.

Make Christ Your Top Priority

Remember Paul's impressive resume?[20] He was a somebody in man's eyes who realized that he was really a nobody in God's eyes until he became somebody in Christ. When his life made a 180 degree turn, he was convinced that his top priority was to know Christ, and he encourages every believer to do the same.

> But whatever was to my profit I now consider loss for the sake of Christ. What is more, I consider everything a loss compared to the surpassing greatness of knowing Christ Jesus my Lord, for whose sake I have lost all things. I consider them rubbish, that I may gain Christ and be found in him, not having a righteousness of my own that comes from the law, but that which is through faith in Christ—the righteousness that comes from God and is by faith. I want to know Christ and the power of his resurrection and the fellowship of sharing in his sufferings, becoming like him in his death. (Philippians 3:7-10)

This is Paul's anthem. It should be our anthem too.

There is nothing greater than knowing Christ. Everything else is trash or waste compared to having Jesus. (The King James Version of the Bible translates the word "rubbish" as "dung!")

God wants you. He chooses you. He made the ultimate sacrifice for you. He doesn't consider you to be the least desirable person like I was when my friends were choosing teams. He considers you to be the most precious thing he has ever created. He does this for all of us. Amazingly, he is big enough to love us all equally. And it is a huge love we share together as followers of Christ.

God has chosen you. He wants you on his side. All you have to do is take the step of faith toward him. Step on the bridge that he has provided in Jesus Christ, and let him be your top priority in life.

For Discussion:

1. Can you recall a time when you were not chosen for something? Did it hurt? Does it still hurt?

2. Consider how God chose King David. Does that story encourage you? Why or why not?

3. How can God take an ordinary life and make it extraordinary?

4. Do you know anyone who was a "nobody" that became a "somebody" in Christ? What about you?

5. Read Philippians 3:7-10 again. What rubbish in your life needs to be removed so that you can be totally committed to knowing Christ?

5

Buried Treasure

Years ago, I had a hankering to buy a metal detector. It would be a great hobby, I thought. Something I could do in my spare time – and possibly make some money selling the buried treasures that I would find. I received some cash as a Christmas present one year so I studied the different types of metal detectors on the market and proceeded to purchase one a week or so after Christmas.

What a waste of money.

I used it only a handful of times. I quickly discovered that this hobby was a lonely and boring activity. I'm used to more exciting things like motorcycling, softball, boating, and golf. I'm not too interested in walking in a lonely field at a pace of six inches per step with my head staring down at the ground.

With the exception of a few coins and bottle caps, I found no treasure. Cliff, my son, received a reward of five dollars with it at the beach when someone who had lost a necklace asked him to search for it near the place where they were sitting. It's the most money my metal detector earned in its short life-span with us until I sold it on eBay a year or so later.

The idea of buried treasure is always intriguing and fascinating. What do you think of when you think of buried treasure? Do you think of Robert Louis Stevenson's *Treasure Island*, Long John Silver, and peg-legged pirates? It is interesting that Scripture deals with this captivating subject.

Jesus said, "The kingdom of heaven is like treasure hidden in a field. When a man found it, he hid it again, and then in his joy went and sold all he had and bought that field."[21]

Jesus recognized the allure and the mystery that always gathers around the notion of hidden treasure. God has his own buried treasures. He speaks of them in this parable.

Burying your valuables in the ground sounds strange to us, but it was a very common practice in the first century. Today, we usually put our money in a bank. We keep our valuables in a safe deposit box. But, in the days of Jesus, there were no banks for the common people. Only wealthy folks had access to banks, which in those days were not very safe places to keep your money anyway. Have you ever heard of wealthy old men who don't trust the banks, so they stuff all their money in their mattress or hide it in scattered stashes throughout their house? That's what the people of the first century did, only they didn't have mattresses; so they buried it.

This was especially true in Palestine because it was a place of frequent warfare. Burying their valuables protected them against any enemies who might raid their homes and try to steal everything.

Jesus told a story about a master who gave some talents (i.e., a measure of money) to his servants. The first servant was given five talents, and the second was given two talents. They invested those amounts and multiplied their master's money. But the third servant, who was given only one talent, was worried. He didn't want anything to happen to that money. He wanted to keep it safe, so what did he do? He buried it in the ground.[22]

Over the years, the ground of Palestine became a veritable treasure house. When the owner of a buried treasure died or was forcefully driven from the land (like during the Babylonian exile), his treasure was lost forever unless someone discovered it. Therefore, it wasn't uncommon at all for a person who was plowing or digging in a field to accidentally come across a treasure. Jesus' parable described a very feasible situation.

There is a concern that readers sometimes have about this parable. At first glance, the man in the parable seems to be dishonest. Honest behavior would demand that this man tell the owner of the field about the treasure since it was on his property and rightfully belonged to him. Right? Not necessarily.

Jewish rabbinic law said, "If a man finds scattered fruit or money, it belongs to the finder." We call that "finders keepers." So the people listening to the parable would not have perceived the man's actions as unethical at all. In fact, the man had a right to what he found. If a man came across money or valuables that were obviously lost and whose owner was dead or unknown, the finder had a right to keep what was found - even if it was found on someone else's property!

It's obvious that the treasure didn't belong to the man who owned the field. If it did, then he would have dug up the treasure before he sold the piece of ground. But he didn't know it was there. Apparently it had belonged to a previous owner, who probably died in battle or by accident, which prevented him from recovering it.

In reality, the man who found the treasure was extremely honest. He didn't have to buy the field. He could have just taken the treasure. But he did not. He bought the field. In fact, he didn't even use the treasure to provide him enough money to make the purchase. Instead, he liquidated everything he owned to come up with the money. The man didn't do anything unethical.

Here's the main point of the parable: A man found something so valuable that he sold everything he had to get it. He was so excited about finding the treasure that he was willing to do whatever he had to do in order to purchase it.

In the back of my Bible, I've written a lot of notes, quotes and verse citations. Many years ago I wrote, "Matthew 13:44 – my testimony" because I could relate this verse to my own story of salvation. I feel like I was that man who discovered this treasure called Jesus. I heard his story. It rattled my cage. I hid it in my heart for awhile and thought about it and investigated the possibilities. Then, I decided to give away all that I had, and I bought into the treasure of salvation that Jesus revealed to me.

Have you discovered God's treasure?

The writer of Proverbs encourages us to seek for God's wisdom as if it is a buried treasure.[23] In Paul's letter to the church in Colosse, he wrote that God's true wisdom is found in Christ.

> My purpose is that they may be encouraged in heart and united in love, so that they may have the full riches of complete understanding, in order that they may know the mystery of God, namely, Christ, in whom are hidden all the treasures of wisdom and knowledge. (Colossians 2:2, 3)

Knowing Christ and all that he offers is a treasure. God desires for you to enjoy the riches that come from knowing and understanding him. This mysterious treasure is found in Jesus. When you discover Jesus and begin to understand his grace, it is like bumping your shovel into a treasure chest full of mystery, wisdom, insight, abundance, and love. The mystery of God and knowing him is unveiled when Christ, God's most precious treasure, is revealed to you.

Christ in You is a Treasure

> I have become its (i.e., the Church's) servant by the commission God gave me to present to you the word of God in its fullness - the mystery that has been kept hidden for ages and generations, but is now disclosed to the saints. To them God has chosen to make known among the Gentiles the glorious riches of this mystery, which is Christ in you, the hope of glory. (Colossians 1:25-27)

Christianity is not about just learning Jesus' teachings and applying them to your life. It's about having Christ in you. Following Jesus is not about going through the motions of religious ritual. It's not about showing up on Sunday mornings and Wednesday nights and clapping and singing and listening and fellowshipping – or even serving. Followers of Buddha and Mohammed do those kinds of things too. If you were to go to a Buddhist temple and observe their services, you would find music, teaching, and fellowship. If you were to go to a mosque and observe a Muslim worship service, you would find music, teaching, and fellowship.

The difference between Christians and other religious people is that we have Christ in us. He lives in you.

1 Corinthians 2:7-10 talks about this secret wisdom that has been hidden and revealed.

> We speak of God's secret wisdom, a wisdom that has been hidden and that God destined for our glory before time began. None of the rulers of this age understood it, for if they had, they would not have crucified the Lord of glory. However, as it is written: "No eye has seen, no ear has heard, no mind has conceived what God has prepared for those who love him" but God has revealed it to us by his Spirit. The Spirit searches all things, even the deep things of God.

God reveals this treasure to us by his Spirit and he hides it within us. "For you died, and your life is now hidden with Christ in God."[24]

Baptism is a symbol of dying and rising again. In New Testament days, when a man was dead and buried, people spoke of him as "hidden in the earth." Paul says that the Christian who died a spiritual death was not hidden in the earth but hidden in Christ.

Chapter 5 – Buried Treasure

Selling It All to Gain the Treasure

> By faith Moses, when he had grown up, refused to be
> known as the son of Pharaoh's daughter. He chose to
> be mistreated along with the people of God rather than
> to enjoy the pleasures of sin for a short time. He
> regarded disgrace for the sake of Christ as of greater
> value than the treasures of Egypt, because he was
> looking ahead to his reward. (Hebrews 11:24-26)

This was a big step of faith for Moses. It must have
brought a lot of ridicule from those who did not know of the
hidden treasure. But it secured his future possession of this
treasure. Moses understood the value of living for God, and he
anticipated his eternal reward.

A wealthy man and his son loved to collect rare works
of art. They had everything in their collection. They would
often sit together and admire the great works of art. The son
went to war. He was very courageous and died in battle while
rescuing another soldier. The father grieved deeply for his
only son.

About a month later, a young man came to his house
with a large package. He said, "Sir, you don't know me, but I
am a soldier that your son died for. He saved many lives that
day, and he was carrying me to safety when a bullet struck
him in the heart and he died instantly. He often talked about
you, and your love for art."

The young man held out his package. "I know this isn't much. I'm not really a great artist, but I think your son would have wanted you to have this."

The father opened the package. It was a portrait of his son, painted by the young man. He stared in awe at the way the soldier had captured the personality of his son in the painting. The father was so drawn to the eyes that his own eyes welled up with tears. He thanked the young man and offered to pay him for the picture. "Oh, no, sir, I could never repay what your son did for me. It's a gift."

The father hung the portrait over his mantle. Every time visitors came to his home, he took them to see the portrait of his son before he showed them any of the other great works he had collected.

When the father died, an auction was held to sell all of his paintings. Many influential people gathered, excited over seeing the great paintings and having an opportunity to purchase one for their collection. The painting of the son sat on the platform. The auctioneer pounded his gavel.

"We will start the bidding with this picture of the son. Who will bid for this picture?" There was silence. Then a voice in the back of the room shouted, "We want to see the famous paintings. Skip this one." But the auctioneer persisted. "Will someone bid for this painting? Who will start the bidding? One hundred dollars? Two hundred dollars?"

Another voice shouted angrily, "We didn't come to see this painting. We came to see the Van Goghs, the Rembrandts, and the Picassos. Get on with the real art!" But still the auctioneer continued. "The son! The son! Who'll take the portrait of the son?" Finally, a voice came from the very back of the room. It was the long-time gardener of the man and his son. "I'll give $10 for the painting." Being a poor man, it was all he could afford.

"We have $10, who will bid $20?"

"Give it to him for $10. Let's see the masters."

"Ten dollars is the bid, won't someone bid twenty?"

The crowd was becoming angry. They didn't want the picture of the son. They wanted the more worthy investments for their collections. The auctioneer pounded the gavel. "Going once, twice, sold for $10!"

A man sitting on the second row shouted. "Now let's get on with the collection!" The auctioneer laid down his gavel. "I'm sorry, the auction is over."

"What about the other paintings?" the crowd was shocked.

"I am sorry. When I was called to conduct this auction, I was told of a secret stipulation in the will. I was not allowed to reveal that stipulation until this time. Only the painting of the son would be auctioned. Whoever bought that painting would inherit the entire estate, including the paintings. The man who takes the son gets everything."

God gave his son Jesus to die on a cross as an expression of his incredible love for us. Like the auctioneer, his message today is, "The son, the son, who'll take the son?"

Because whoever takes the Son gets everything.

A.W. Tozer wrote, "The man who has God for his treasure has all things in One. Many ordinary treasures may be denied him, or if he is allowed to have them, the enjoyment of them will be so tempered that they will never be necessary to his happiness. Or if he must see them go, one after one, he will scarcely feel a sense of loss, for having the Source of all things he has in Him all satisfaction, all pleasure, all delight. Whatever he may lose he has actually lost nothing, for he now has it all in One (Christ), and he has it purely legitimately and forever."[25]

In other words, when you have Christ, you have it all. This is why the things of the world will never satisfy you. We have a valuable treasure. Don't ever forget it.

For Discussion:

1. Have you ever uncovered a treasure? Tell about it.
2. What do you treasure most in your life?
3. What do others seem to treasure most in life?
4. What is the difference between Christianity and other religions according to this chapter?
5. Look at Hebrews 11:24-26. What does this passage say about sin? What does it say about pursuing Christ?

Laughing with Sarah

In 1926, the man whose invention would ultimately produce the television tube made an interesting statement: "Television is an impossibility - commercially and financially. It's not worth our dreaming." Today, almost every home in America has at least one TV set.

In 1945, a naval officer said, "The thing will never go off. It's the biggest fool mistake we've ever made. The atomic bomb will not explode. I ought to know, because I'm an expert in explosives." On August 6, 1945, an atomic bomb destroyed Hiroshima, Japan.

In 1948, a respected science magazine commented, "Landing and moving around the moon involves so many problems that it may well take scientists another 200 years." On July 20, 1969, Neil Armstrong planted his left foot on the surface of the moon.

Around 2000 BC, God told Abraham that his old, barren wife, Sarah, would have a son. Sarah was listening to the conversation between the Lord and Abraham. When she heard this, she laughed and said, "I'm worn out. I'm married to an old man. Now I'm going to have a child? Puh-leaze!"[26]

Sometimes the promises of God seem beyond belief, and the only human response is a bitter, sarcastic laugh. Just as scientists, inventors, and journalists, scoffed at TV, the atomic bomb, and landing on the moon, so sometimes when men hear God promise something impossible, they laugh uncontrollably.

In the New Testament, Abraham and Sarah are pictured as heroes of the faith, but in Genesis they both laughed at the prospect of Sarah bearing a child.[27]

Their story honestly portrays the difficulty of faith. It is a comfort to me that the Bible often pictures the great ancestors of the faith not as models of belief, but as examples of disbelief. It reminds us that faith does not always come to us reasonably and carefully measured by some scientist in a white lab coat. Faith can't be put under a microscope. Sometimes faith demands that we believe a couple of wrinkled old-timers are going to have a baby or that God will lead his people out of bondage in Egypt or that a virgin will conceive and bear a son or that one crucified as a criminal will rise from the dead as the Savior of mankind.

Is Anything Too Hard for God?

The whole story of Abraham and Sarah revolves around the question God asks when Sarah's laughter finally dies down, "Is anything too hard for the Lord?"[28] It is not an affirmation or a proclamation, but a question. It comes as a question because faith requires a decision. This question demands an answer from us.

We tend to answer this question one of two ways. First, we are too quick and superficial with our reply. For those who have been faithful all of their lives, it is more of a rhetorical question rather than a real question. We've heard all the stories before, so we reply like a kid in Sunday School wildly waving his hand, "No, of course not! Nothing is impossible with God!"

Some may answer this question too quickly in another way: "Yes, some things are impossible, even for God - if there is a God." That is the answer many people in our current culture would offer. Those who answer in this way have reduced this mysterious universe into a closed system of cause and effect. God is no longer Almighty God - benevolent, maybe; kind and concerned, perhaps - but ultimately powerless to make a difference in the world. Everything is involved in a chain of events based on natural and universal laws, and we, as human beings, merely ride out this series of happenings doing the best we possibly can to survive.

Chapter 6 – Laughing with Sarah

Though nearly 4000 years ago, this was the world that Abraham and Sarah lived in, too. A world where you came to terms with barrenness at 90 years old.

If we answer God's question too quickly, we may miss his point. This question forces us to a deep reflection of what we really believe about God. Our entire view of life depends on how we answer it.

If we answer the question by saying, "No, nothing is impossible for God" - and mean it - then we have a whole new view of life. Anything can happen. The possibilities are staggering! The world suddenly becomes a place where old women have babies, slaves march through the Red Sea, and the dead rise again.

It's interesting to note that Abraham and Sarah left God's question unanswered. It's a tough one to answer. It could be one of the most important questions you will ever consider.

The Hebrew root word for "too hard" in the passage noted above means "impossible, too difficult" or even "too wonderful." We normally don't make the comparison between the words wonderful and impossible. This word pops up again and again in Scripture. Exodus 15 is an example. Miriam dances in triumph, slapping her thigh with her tambourine because God had delivered the Hebrew slaves through the Red Sea. She sings, "Who among the gods is like you, o Lord? Who is like you - majestic in holiness, awesome in glory, working wonders," i.e., doing the impossible.[29]

Later in the Old Testament, an angel visits Manoah, Samson's father, to announce Samson's birth to his barren wife. Manoah wants to make sure this comes from the highest authority in heaven. He asks, "What did you say your name was?" The angel replied, "Why do you ask? Just call me wonderful" (i.e., impossible).30

The word occurs often in the Psalms. Whenever they sing praises of God who does "marvelous" or "wonderful" works, it is the same word. Israel praised God for doing wonderful impossibilities, and they are often warned not to forget his wonderful works.

The subject of impossibilities makes its way into the New Testament. When the angel visits Mary to announce her pregnancy, he also announces the pregnancy of Elizabeth, who, like Sarah, is very old. "Even Elizabeth your relative is going to have a child in her old age, and she who was said to be barren is in her sixth month, for nothing is impossible with God."31

Jesus takes up the same question in Mark 10. When he describes the difficulty of discipleship, the disciples balk at how hard it is. Jesus said, "With men it is impossible, but not with God; for all things are possible with God" (v. 27).

In Matthew 17, Jesus rebuked the disciples for their inability to cast out a demon. He said, "Truly, I tell you, if you have faith the size of a mustard seed, you will say to this mountain, 'Move from here to there,' and it will move; and nothing will be impossible for you" (v. 20). When we have faith, when we rely on God, then truly nothing is impossible, not only for God, but for us.

The question of what is possible for God and for believers then has been answered. Everything is possible! Nothing is impossible!

Is that really true?

Are we given a blank check from the New Jerusalem Bank and Trust Company when we become believers? Can we control the impossibilities in our lives? Some people say so. Some teach that if you believe hard enough, you'll receive anything from financial security to physical healing. There is even a book titled *How to Write Your Own Ticket with God*. According to this theology, God is like a trained dolphin that jumps when we say jump through impossible hoops at the snap of our fingers.

Can we control the impossibilities in our life? Can we write our own ticket with God if we have enough faith? I don't think so. God is the one who performs the impossibilities and Abraham and Sarah make it clear that he doesn't need our faith to do so. We have to remember that the impossibility granted to Abraham and Sarah was not just any impossibility. It was an impossibility that fulfilled God's will and purpose.

This becomes clearer when we look at one more instance where the word that has to do with impossibilities occurs. In Mark 14, Jesus lies prostrate on the ground in the garden of Gethsemane the night before his crucifixion. He was praying to be delivered from that hour of pain and torment.

He prayed, "Abba," (which literally means Daddy) "Father, everything is possible for you. Take this cup from me. Yet not what I will, but what you will" (v. 36).

Maybe we've answered God's question to Abraham. There is at least one thing that is impossible for God: It is impossible for God to go back on his will and purpose to save men through the suffering of his Son. Obedience without a cross, salvation without death on the cross, sanctification without propitiation for sin on the cross, new birth without death to the old self, these are impossible with God. Someone had to bridge the gap between sinful man and holy God - there is no other way.

Jesus told his disciples, trying to prepare them for his death that, "Unless a grain of wheat falls into the ground and dies, it remains only a single seed. But if it dies, it produces many seeds."[32] Jesus didn't seem to think that we could write our own ticket with God. His was a nonrefundable ticket to the cross.

You see, the secret to this question is not whether or not God can do the impossible. Of course he can do the impossible. The secret is: Is it God's will? That is the impossibility. It is impossible for God not to do his will.

What Jesus illustrated that night in Gethsemane was that resurrection will come, but first you have to go "through the valley of the shadow of death." You can become a new creation, but first, you have to let old things pass away.

We all have pains, failures, sickness, and doubts. It may even be that you, like Sarah, are barren. In these difficulties we ask ourselves the question "Is anything too hard for God?" When an innocent child dies from cancer on a Christmas morning, it takes on a whole new meaning. Was it impossible for God to banish this cancer from her body? Of course not. But the issue is not one of possibilities or impossibilities. The issue is, "Is it God's will for this person, for this world, for this time, for this place?"

We can leave God's will confidently in his loving hands, just as Jesus did that night in the garden.

> Now the Lord was gracious to Sarah as he had said, and the Lord did for Sarah what he had promised. Sarah became pregnant and bore a son to Abraham in his old age, at the very time God had promised him. Abraham gave the name Isaac to the son Sarah bore him. When his son Isaac was eight days old, Abraham circumcised him, as God commanded him. Abraham was a hundred years old when his son Isaac was born to him. Sarah said, "God has brought me laughter, and everyone who hears about this will laugh with me." And she added, "Who would have said to Abraham that Sarah would nurse children? Yet I have borne him a son in his old age." (Genesis 21:1-7)

Abraham and Sarah, along with Jesus, discovered that the answer to this question may follow slow and painful waiting. It requires faithful patience. It may include long, dark nights where it seems you've been abandoned. It may not even become clear until that "great gettin' up morning." But the story of the Bible tells us the ultimate answer to the question, "Is anything too hard for God?" and like the little child faithfully answers in Sunday School, we can say, "No! Nothing is impossible with God." Because in God's time, Isaac, the child of laughter, is born. The slaves are set free by a splitting sea. The crucified one is resurrected on Easter morning. That is why we can, in faith, sing the praise of God for whom nothing is impossible.

He is able. He is able to take our worries and our woes. He is able to turn our pain into pleasure. He is able to take our failures and turn them into accomplishments. He is able to take our infirmities and make us vigorous. He is able to turn our doubts into firm conviction.

There is one other seemingly impossibility that you should know. He is able to take our sinfulness and turn us into new creations. He is able to turn sinners into saints. He is able to give eternal life to dying men. If you will acknowledge Jesus' incredible act of grace and be born again, then you can inherit the kingdom of God. "Unless one is born again, he cannot see the kingdom of God."[33]

"Without faith it is impossible to please God because anyone who comes to him must believe that he exists and that he rewards those who earnestly seek him."[34]

Once you make the decision to live for Christ, anything is possible. He is able to deliver you from any and all circumstances according to his will. As the king told Daniel when he was thrown into the lion's den, "Your God, whom you constantly serve, will himself deliver you."[35]

For Discussion:

1. What modern day conveniences do we take for granted that were once considered impossible?

2. Are you quick to be skeptical of a far-fetched plan or are you willing to give difficult things a try?

3. The foundation of the Christian faith is based on "impossibility," i.e., the resurrection of Christ. Why, then, is it so hard for us to believe other seemingly impossible things?

4. How does knowing that God can do the impossible change your day-to-day journey with him?

5. Read Hebrews 11:6. What is impossible to do according to this verse?

7

His Hands

The hand is an amazing tool. It can gently cradle an infant. It can grip a baseball and hurl it at over 90 mph. It can repair the tiny mechanisms of a fine watch. It can support the whole weight of a rock climber by the grip of the fingertips wedged into a small crack in the rock.

It is composed of 27 bones and 38 muscles. It can perform incredible tasks. It is a marvelous machine at the end of our appendages called arms. With the thumb appropriately positioned, we can grasp things. With the fingernails, we pick up flat objects like coins. With sensitive nerves on our fingertips, we can evaluate the texture and temperature of the world around us. The human hand is truly "fearfully and wonderfully made" - manufactured by God himself.

What do you think of when you look at your hands? There is history in your hands. I see a few scars on mine. A scar from where I punched a boy in the mouth in the eighth grade only to connect with his teeth and cut my knuckle. There are two little blue spots on my fingers where a freshly sharpened pencil was jabbed into my hand. I have a couple of scars from playing football. I look at the ring finger of my left hand and I am reminded of my wonderful bride and the commitment we made many years ago. In my early 30's, I broke my right hand playing basketball. I learned how valuable it was as I had to manage life with a cast for a month or so. I'm sure you have a few memories stored away in your hands too.

Before he began making sausages, Jimmy Dean had a country song called *These Hands*.

These hands ain't the hands of a gentleman,
These hands are calloused and worn.
These hands raised a family,
These hands raised a home,
Now these hands raise to praise the Lord.

These hands won the heart of my loved one,
And with hers they were never alone,
So if these hands do their task,
Then what more could one ask,
For these fingers have worked to the bone.

Now I'm tired and I'm old and I ain't got much gold,

Maybe things ain't been all that I planned,

But Lord above, hear my plea

When it's time to judge me,

Take a look at these hard-workin' hands.

The hand is indeed an incredible creation. It is even more amazing when we consider the hands of Jesus. Jesus touched many lives - literally. A touch from the Master's hand has changed many people - and he still touches lives today.

A brief journey through the Gospels reveals the work of Jesus' hands. The first reference to the hands of Jesus is found in Matthew 8 where Jesus had a large crowd following him. A man with leprosy came to him and said, "Lord, if you are willing, make me clean." Jesus reached out his hand and touched the man saying, "I am willing. Be clean." Immediately, he was cured of leprosy.[36]

The first thing that Jesus did was the last thing anyone would have dreamed of doing. According to the law of those days, to touch a leper meant defilement and social death. It was an abomination to touch or even go near a leper. But Jesus is different. He is the Great Physician. He stretched out his hands, touched the leper, and the leper was never the same after the touch from Jesus.

Had Jesus been a mere man, to touch the leper would have been to defile himself. But because he was God in the flesh the touch did not defile him but rather caused the leper to be undefiled.

Later in the same chapter of the book of Matthew, we read where Jesus arrived at Peter's house. Peter's mother-in-law was lying in bed sick with a fever. Jesus touched her hand, the fever left her, and she got up and began to serve Jesus. There was a supernatural energy produced through Jesus' hand that brought about an immediate cure.[37]

Later in Matthew's gospel, we read where Jesus was approached by a synagogue official who knelt before him and said, "My daughter has just died. But you can put your hand on her and she will live." Jesus went to the man's house to find that they had already begun the funeral. He told them to go away and that the girl was not dead. But they laughed at him. The crowd left the house anyway, and Jesus went in and took the girl by the hand and she got up. The Bible says that the news of her recovery spread throughout the region.[38]

When Jesus left there, he was being followed by two blind men who were calling out to him, "Have mercy on us, Son of David!" Jesus looked at them and said, "Do you believe that I am able to do this?" "Yes, Lord," they replied. Then he touched their eyes and said, "Because of your faith it will be done." Immediately their sight was restored.[39]

The Bible records many other instances where Jesus' touch restored the health of others. In the book of Mark, some people brought a blind man to Jesus and begged him to touch him. The Bible says that Jesus spit on the man's eyes, put his hands on the man's eyes twice, and the man was no longer blind.[40]

Once as Jesus was entering a small town, a funeral procession was coming out of the city. The dead person being carried out was the only son of his mother who was a widow. A large crowd from the town was with her. Jesus saw her and it broke his heart. He went to her and said, "Don't cry." Then he went up to the coffin, touched it, and ordered, "Young man, get up!" The once dead man sat up and began to talk, and the crowd rejoiced.[41]

Jesus touched the blind, and they could see. Jesus touched the sick, and they were made whole. Jesus touched the dead, and they were resurrected.

On one occasion he was teaching to more than 5000 people. He had gone out to a remote location for some time to be alone, but the crowds discovered where he was and followed him. He healed those who had come to him, and, as evening approached, the disciples came to him and said, "Lord, we're out here in the middle of nowhere. Send the crowd away so that they can go home and get some food."

Jesus said, "They don't need to go away. Let's just feed them right here."

"All we have is five loaves of bread and two fish!" they said.

"Bring it here," Jesus said. When they brought the meager meal to Jesus, he took it in his hands and looked up to heaven, gave thanks, then broke the bread. Everyone ate - 5000 men plus women and children with twelve baskets of leftovers.[42]

One night the disciples were out fishing on the Sea of Galilee when they saw someone walking on the water toward them. They were afraid. They thought it was a ghost. Peter knew that it was Jesus. He got out of the boat and began walking on the water toward Jesus. When Peter realized what he was doing, he became afraid and began to sink. He cried out to Jesus, "Lord, save me!" Immediately, Jesus reached out his hand and caught him. They walked back together to the boat.[43]

Jesus loves children. Matthew's book tells us that people would bring their children to Jesus, and he would place his hands on them and pray for them.

Jesus loves people. He loves lepers and prostitutes. He loves rulers and peasants. He loves the religious and irreligious. He even loved Judas, the disciple who betrayed him. As he sat with his disciples at the Last Supper, he said of Judas, "The hand of my betrayer is with my hand on this table."[44]

On the night of Jesus' arrest, he was praying in the Garden of Gethsemane just across the valley from Jerusalem. When the authorities came to arrest him, Peter tried to take matters in his own hands. He drew a sword and slashed the ear of the high priest's servant. Jesus said, "There will be no more of this." With that, he touched the ear of the servant, his enemy, and the man was healed.[45]

But Jesus did even greater things with his hands

After Jesus was arrested, it was determined that he should be crucified - perhaps one of the worst forms of capital punishment known to man.

Prior to his crucifixion, Jesus' hands were tied to a whipping post. While tied to this post, the Roman soldiers bent him over and scourged him. To be scourged meant to be beaten over and over with leather whips. But these weren't ordinary whips. At the end of each whip were sharp pieces of bone, steel, and glass. Each strike against Jesus' back literally tore the flesh bringing severe pain and agony. Many crucifixion victims of that day never made it to the cross. The scourging alone was enough to cause death.

After they scourged him, they untied his hands from the whipping post, stripped him, and placed a purple robe on him. Then someone twisted together a crown of thorns and pressed it onto his head. They took his right hand and placed a staff in it. They began to kneel before him and mock him and laugh at him. The Roman soldiers sarcastically worshipped him saying, "Hail, King of the Jews."

They spit on him and struck him in the face again and again. Then they led him away to be crucified.

The soldiers spread out Jesus' hands and tied them to a crossbeam. Once the crossbeam was tied to his hands, they led him toward a place outside the walls of Jerusalem called Golgotha. Some historians say it was the city dump. On the way out of the city, the soldiers forced a man named Simon to help Jesus to the place of his execution.

When they got there, they laid him down and attached the crossbeam to another beam that would be the upright part of the cross. They stretched out his hands and nailed them to the cross. After both hands were nailed, they nailed his feet to the cross as well.

A hole in the ground had been prepared prior to the crucifixion. The soldiers lifted up the cross, lined up the bottom of the cross with the hole, and dropped the cross into the earth with the whole body weight of the Lord crashing down with it.

He hung there supported only by nails in his hands and feet and perhaps a small peg between his legs. Needless to say, Jesus was in tremendous agony. The nails, the scourging, the crown of thorns pressed into his head, and a fever - often produced by crucifixion, brought unbearable pain. The abnormal position of his body created additional torture.

But the worst pain of all was the pain of being separated from God. For it was on the cross that Jesus Christ became the sacrificial lamb - the bearer of all of men's sin. As he hung on the cross, Jesus cried out, "My God! My God! Why have you forsaken me?"[46]

2 Corinthians 5:21 says, "God made him who had no sin to be sin for us, so that in him we might become the righteousness of God."

Jesus took on the sin of us all. When he bore our sin, God, in his holiness and purity, could not be present. Because

God cannot be in the presence of sin, he had to separate himself from Jesus.

Jesus spread out his hands for you and me - taking on the sins of the past, present, and future.

When Jesus came to the end, he knew where to place his hope. He said, "Father, into your hands I commit my spirit." After he said this, he breathed his last breath.[47]

Jesus hung by his hands on the cross so that we might turn from our own selfish, sinful, destructive ways, beg for God's forgiveness and cleansing for our sins, and place our full faith and trust in him for eternity.

Peter later wrote, "For Christ died for sins once for all, the righteous for the unrighteous, to bring you to God."[48]

He hung by his hands on the cross so that you and I might know him and experience a full and abundant life both now and forever. All we have to do is receive the gift of salvation that Jesus has provided for us.

We have two options. The Bible says that if we choose not to receive the gift that Christ has provided for us, "It is a dreadful thing to fall into the hands of the living God."[49]

If we choose Christ, we are promised that we will never be snatched from his hand. "My sheep listen to my voice; I know them, and they follow me. I give them eternal life, and they shall never perish; no one can snatch them out of my hand. My Father, who has given them to me, is greater than all; no one can snatch them out of my Father's hand."[50]

It should have been my hands. It should have been my feet. But Jesus paid the price for me. He took matters into his own hands.

So I've handed my life over to him.

For Discussion:

1. Look at your hands. What stories do they tell?
2. There is power in the human touch. Why do you think that is so? Why is it important to be touched?
3. After Jesus touched the people whom he healed, what were their reactions? How do you suppose you would have reacted?
4. The crucifixion is a disturbing scene. What part of the crucifixion story touches you most?
5. The Church is supposed to be the hands and feet of Jesus. What can you do with your hands this week to demonstrate Christ's love to others?

8

The Dynamite Box

Author Calvin Miller wrote about an antique wooden dynamite box in his home. The box was made in the 19th century. It was carefully constructed to withstand shock as its explosive contents were transported from the manufacturer to its place of use.

On the lid were large red and black letters which said, "DANGER DYNAMITE!" But Miller wrote that the last time he saw it, it was filled with a bunch of junk in his workshop.

Like Calvin Miller's antique dynamite box, Christians are built specifically to transport God's power into the world. But, if we're not careful, we will clutter our lives with so many other things that we will lose our power, passion, and enthusiasm. Our spiritual power will be nonexistent.

What image comes to mind when you think of enthusiasm? I think of cheerleaders, motivational speakers, or super salesmen. It is often something we try to conjure up in ourselves or others. Enthusiasm seems at times superficial like a mood we create to get us past the next challenge. For some, enthusiasm comes naturally. It's part of their DNA.

I believe everyone should be enthusiastic because the word enthusiasm means "God in you." The Greek construction of this word is the prefix "en" which means "with or in" and "theos" means God. If you have God in your life, you have enthusiasm i.e., en-theos.

How do you maintain your enthusiasm for the Lord? How do you keep your life from being filled up with clutter like the dynamite box? How does someone generate enough enthusiasm to build an ark the size of a football field like Noah, or slay a nine-foot tall giant like David?

Do you ever feel like you are doing more and more and enjoying it less and less? There are a lot of weary Christians out there. You do more, know more, and take on more things, but you're not really making any progress. As time goes by, you suffer from spiritual weariness. You get tired of being spiritually frustrated and quit, or you just travel numbly back and forth to church with no real intentions of improving your walk with the Lord but ashamed to admit it.

You've lost your enthusiasm.

You may fall into this category. I'm not talking about stress or burnout. It's deeper than that. It's better described as spiritual fatigue. What began as an exciting pilgrimage with the Lord has degenerated into a rat race.

And the rats are winning.

How do you get your spiritual enthusiasm back? Some would say enthusiasm is generated by going to large meetings or conferences and hearing great singers and speakers in a packed auditorium or concert hall. Some would say that you've got to get out and be exposed to the real world and see the needs of real people. Go work in a soup kitchen or homeless shelter. Become a counselor at the local Crisis Pregnancy Center and talk with young girls bent on aborting their babies. You'll get passion quickly.

Others would suggest that you go on a mission trip. See the world and the incredible volumes of people who don't know Jesus - that'll fire you up.

There is merit and truth in all of these things. The problem is - where do you find the enthusiasm to sign up? The fact is that many Christians have pursued all of these methods but still wrestle with a lack of spiritual enthusiasm. These things might work at first, but, over time, they become a burden to bear rather than a joy to share.

Pastors and church leaders constantly wrestle with this problem. How can we keep our members continuously enthusiastic? This is why churches have program after program, event after event, class after class, concert after concert. They have a 13-week course on a subject that is sure to fire up the troops. By the time the course is over, everyone is tired of it and ready to move on to something else. So they jump into another course. It is a continuous cycle. The pastor holds a carrot on a stick in front of his flock to make them run, and they run because they think the next great program will generate enthusiasm.

Maybe we just don't know what we are looking for when we talk about enthusiasm. What does an enthusiastic Christian look like? Is he/she a well-known hero, athlete, author, speaker, musician, organizational head, CEO, or pastor? Some think so because these kinds of people tend to be our role models.

I heard a popular mega-church pastor declare that God wants us all to be eagles. According to this pastor, God wants us to soar high, have wealth, influence, and power. I know what the Scriptures say about eagles[51] and I know that the pastor was trying to inspire people to be all that they can be. But I also had to ask as I listened to the famous preacher, "Does God really want everyone to be an eagle? Doesn't he want some to be sparrows, wrens, robins, or woodpeckers? Wouldn't it be boring if everyone was an eagle?"

Most believers are common, ordinary men and women who live routine lives - making a home for the family, coping as a single, trying to get or keep a job, nursing along a tired automobile they can't afford to replace, concerned about retirement, and wondering whether or not they're going to amount to anything. They will never be rich, famous, or powerful. What does an enthusiastic, passionate Christian look like in this context?

In 1 Chronicles 11, there is an obscure story that recalls a time in David's life when he found himself in hostile conditions. He was forced to flee to the desert to survive. His enemy was the Philistines. They were strong and, at the moment, they were victorious against David's people. At the time of this story, the Philistines held strong positions around Bethlehem, David's original hometown.

> Three of the thirty chiefs came down to David to the rock at the cave of Adullam, while a band of Philistines was encamped in the Valley of Rephaim. At that time David was in the stronghold, and the Philistine garrison was at Bethlehem. David longed for water and said, "Oh, that someone would get me a drink of water from the well near the gate of Bethlehem!" So the Three broke through the Philistine lines, drew water from the well near the gate of Bethlehem and carried it back to David. But he refused to drink it; instead, he poured it out before the Lord. "God forbid that I should do this!" he said. "Should I drink the blood of these men who went at the risk of their lives?" Because they risked their lives to bring it back, David would not drink it. Such were the exploits of the three mighty men. (1 Chronicles 11:15-19)

Thirty certain men of Israel had drifted into the hills to join David who formed a kind of guerilla army. These men were loyal and devoted to David. You can assume that David was tired of running, tired of living in caves, and probably tired of being at war. In a quiet moment, David spoke of the good old days and said, "Oh, I would love to have some water from the well near the gate of Bethlehem."

It is important to understand that David's statement was not a command, just a wish. But David's men were so loyal that when they heard it and knew that it would bring pleasure to their king, they immediately determined that they would get him a drink of water from the well at the gate of Bethlehem.

The trio set out to fight their way against the Philistines breaking through enemy lines to get water for David. They risked their lives for a drink of water! David knew devotion when he saw it. Therefore, when they presented it to him, he poured it out as an offering to the Lord because he knew that no human being was worthy of such a gift.

The three men were obviously passionate for their king.

Intimacy with the King

The fact is that David uttered this wish quietly and informally. It was not an official pronouncement. It was not a royal command. It was just something that he hadn't enjoyed in a long while. Here's the key. You had to be in the presence of the king to have heard it. The 27 other men were probably doing rather routine things when David uttered these words - pitching tents, shining boots, cooking, sharpening weapons, etc. - all good and necessary things. But the best thing to do was to be in the presence of the king where not only commands could be heard, but also a few wishes.

If you want to regain your enthusiasm for the Lord, you need to spend time with him listening to what he says and seeking to do the things that please him. Paul the apostle wrote, "We make it our goal to please him."[52] The Bible is full of passages indicating that we are to please God in all we do. We are to be God-pleasers.

To know how to please God, we must spend time with him. Ignoring this fact leads to spiritual weariness and lack of enthusiasm.

It's no different than any other relationship. If I intend to know my wife's wishes and desires, I need to spend time with her. If I want to know my children's dreams and plans, I have to spend time with them. In order to know my Lord's thinking, I have to spend time with him and please him in all that I do.

Willing to Take a Risk

The account of this story doesn't include any debate among the three men. Imagine the dialogue among the three of them. "Are you crazy? Do you know where that well is and how strong the Philistines have fortified that area? Do you know how many men we'll have to mow down to get there? For a drink of water?"

It may be that this is not recorded because it didn't happen. The purpose of the story is to show how enthusiastic, devoted, passionate people really think and act. The wish of the king came across like a command to the devoted.

When you are convicted from a genuine encounter with the king, it creates enthusiasm. Enthusiasm leads to action.

When Moses heard the Lord speak from the burning bush, he raised a few questions about it, but he left with enough enthusiasm to lead a whole nation to the Promised Land. When Mary heard from God through an angel, she was surprised and scared, but she was moved to action. When Paul heard the Lord speak on the Damascus road, he was so enthusiastic that he became the leader of the New Testament church movement.

When you hear from the King, you are willing to take a risk and take action.

Divine Energy

Throughout the Bible, we read of this mysterious energy or power that comes from God. When his power is planted within his people, amazing things happen. We know that divine energy or power to be the Holy Spirit.

Acts 17:6 tells us that Spirit-led disciples turned the world upside down for Christ.[53] Through the centuries, common and somewhat unskilled people have caused remarkable things to happen in their worlds when the passion of God invaded them. They took risks, overcame obstacles, and set standards that leave us breathless.

This is what happens when the Spirit of God fills us. The spiritually weary person becomes alive and powerful. When we are filled and led by the Holy Spirit, we are truly enthusiastic.

We have God in us.

But how are we to be filled with the Holy Spirit? What steps do we take? First of all, we develop intimacy with the Lord. Spend time with the King - listening and learning. Second, we act on what he tells us - even if it's at a risk! Third, we rely on his divine energy and power. Ephesians 5:18 commands us to be filled with the Holy Spirit. What can we do to be filled?

Jesus gives us a clue in his famous sermon on the mount. "Blessed are those who hunger and thirst for righteousness, for they will be filled."[54]

The spiritually hungry and thirsty will be filled. "How can I make myself hungry and thirsty for righteousness?" you might ask. A church in Ephesus had that problem. Jesus told them, "Yet I hold this against you: You have forsaken your first love. Remember the height from which you have fallen! Repent and do the things you did at first."[55]

Jesus told them to do the 3 R's...remember, repent, and repeat.

Remember the joy of your salvation. Remember the enthusiasm. Remember what has brought you this far. "Remember the early days after you received the light."[56]

Repent. Take a U turn.

That's all it really means. Repent means to turn away from self-seeking, self-centered living and focus on selfless, graceful living with Christ as your goal and role model. To repent simply means to turn from spiritually unproductive things.

Repeat. Do the things you did at first - when you were spiritually hungry and thirsty.

Once I became a Christ-follower, I can recall spending hours reading and getting to know him through the Scriptures. I read other books about Christian living, met with other believers for Bible study, and spoke about it often with faithful friends. I was hungry to know Christ.

There are periods in the journey when that hunger wanes, however. There are seasons when I don't have the same passion and desire to know Christ like I should. When I need to be reinvigorated, I have to go back to the basics and do the things that I did at first. Now, having spent three decades with Christ, I can flip through my Bible and see underlined verses, study notes that I've written in the margins, and quotes from lessons I've heard over the years. Just a quick journey through my Bible helps me to remember, repent, and repeat.

Practicing the 3 R's gives you the divine energy from God that empowers us to do his will on a daily basis. It's a matter of focus. Enthusiasm comes when we focus on his incredible grace and love. Enthusiasm leaves when we get sucked into the daily concerns of life.

The Oil Next Door

Imagine that you live next to a beautiful field and suppose that one of your neighbors secretly hates you. He is dedicated to hurting you and ruining your life. Your enemy knows that this beautiful piece of land is for sale and in addition to that, this land has oil underground. He cannot afford to purchase the land himself, but, because he hates you so much, he is determined to do everything possible to prevent you from buying it. One day, however, he is caught off guard, you discover the land is for sale and buy it.

Your enemy is furious that you've bought the property, but he cannot change the fact. However, his hatred for you is so obsessive that he decides he will do everything possible to prevent you from ever learning that there is oil on the property. One strategy he employs is to keep you occupied with all kinds of activities – social gatherings, ball games, meetings, concerts, and other events. He believes that if you are busy enough on the surface, you will never discover the oil that is underneath. If that doesn't work, he can try to divert you with all kinds of legal regulations and bureaucratic red tape that will bog you down and keep you from doing anything productive with the land.

Whatever his methods, if he succeeds, your enemy will have done almost as much harm as if he had actually prevented you from buying the land in the first place.

That is what the Enemy tries to do with us. Once we become children of God, Satan has lost that most important battle. Now his only weapon against us is to try and fill our lives with apathy, ritual, religion, and busyness. He wants to take away our enthusiasm so that we never discover the incredible wealth that we have inherited as children of the living God.

Don't let him do that to you! Spend time with the King. Listen and act with Holy Spirit power. Remember what it was like when you first fell in love with Jesus. Repent from the sinful habits in your life and repeat the things you did early in your Christian walk that fired you up.

You are designed to transport God's power into this world. You have been gifted to make a difference. You have been crafted by the Creator to influence others for Christ. Don't become a dynamite box full of junk. Be filled with his power and make an impact on the world around you.

For Discussion:

1. What image comes to your mind when you think of enthusiasm?
2. Would other people consider you enthusiastic about your faith?
3. Have you ever experienced spiritual burnout?
4. How do you maintain your enthusiasm for Christ?
5. How can you put the 3 R's in practice each day?

9

Is It in You?

August is the official beginning of football season. In the South, that means hot, humid, and exhausting sessions that result in cottonmouth, a condition when your mouth is so dry that it looks and feels like there is cotton inside. There were times when I thought I would die from thirst in those days. Fights would break out among players cutting in line when given the chance to run to the water cooler for some relief. I remember coming home from football practices and going straight to the bathroom and sticking my head under the bathroom faucet to drink until I was nearly sick. For some reason, the water that came out of the bathroom sink tasted better and seemed colder.

When you hydrate a dehydrated body, your body's need for water is satisfied. Your body gets back in order and right with your body's chemistry. Gatorade's slogan is, "Is it in you?" When you drink Gatorade, it helps satisfy some of the body's basic needs by providing water, carbohydrates, and electrolytes back into your system.

I guess you could say hydrating your body makes it happy.

The word "blessed" means happy. In fact, it means "very, very happy." The first Psalm talks about the life of a blessed man and how he can live a prosperous life. Do you have what it takes to live a blessed, happy, and prosperous life? Is it in you? It is if you live according to Psalm 1. It tells us the keys to a happy life.

Keep Your Distance from Sin

Blessed is the man who does not walk in the counsel of the wicked or stand in the way of sinners or sit in the seat of mockers. (Psalm 1:1)

Note the progression of how sin works in our lives. The Psalmist describes three scenarios. First, we begin walking along side those who are naturally wicked. The wicked are those who are without God. They are guided and controlled by their own desires, emotions, and impulses. Second, we stand in the sinner's path – a well-worn behavior pattern that has entrenched them in their negative conduct. To stand with someone rather than walking along side them generally means you're having a more intense and serious conversation. The third scenario describes sitting down in the seat of mockers. Sitting down implies a much deeper level of kinship than walking with or even standing with someone. To sit down with a mocker means that you are involved and comfortable with the worst of sinners. A mocker has no regard for God, makes light of God, and puts down the things of God.

This verse warns us how we are prone to turn aside little by little and become more and more entangled in the web of sin. We are easily influenced by the ways of the world.

It does not suggest that we shouldn't hang out with these people. If you're going to have an impact on the world and if you're going to live in the world, you have to hang out with people who don't know God. It warns against taking their advice. Instead of receiving counsel from the sinner, get your wisdom from God. Don't go down the same path with them, and don't get involved in the wrong things that they may do.

You may ask, "Aren't these the people we are trying to influence for God? Aren't these people in need of Jesus? Aren't we supposed to be out in the culture influencing people to be Christ-followers?" Yes, definitely yes. But be aware of who is influencing whom. When you begin to take the counsel of those who do not know God and go down the same path as those who deliberately choose against God's ways and sit down with the mocker and make light of the things of God, who is influencing whom?

We have to be careful to keep our distance from sin. Why? Because sin dehydrates you. It causes your spiritual life to dry up. It brings withering and decay. It causes you to be fruitless instead of fruitful.

Delight in God's Teaching

> "But his delight is in the law of the Lord, and on his law he meditates day and night." (Psalm 1:2)

What if your dad was the smartest, greatest dad in the history of the world? What if he wrote a book containing everything you need to know in order to live a blessed and happy life? Would you read it? Of course, you would.

Guess what? He did. Your heavenly Father has written such a book.

We often don't delight and meditate on God and his teachings because our lives are too noisy. God often speaks in the silence when we are totally focused on him with no distractions. But if we don't make room for God to speak in our lives, how will we hear from him?

Psalm 1 says that in order to be blessed or happy, we must delight in God's teaching and meditate on it day and night. But we have to carve time out of our lives in order to hear from God. You can't meditate in a noisy environment. You have to create time in your life for silence, meditation, and listening to God. You've got to slow it down, get the noise out of your life, and pay attention to what God is trying to teach you.

It's been said that a Bible that is worn and falling apart from use usually belongs to someone who isn't. Dwight L. Moody said, "I never saw a useful Christian who was not a student of the Bible."

Prosper with God's Teaching

He is like a tree planted by streams of water, which yields its fruit in season and whose leaf does not wither. Whatever he does prospers. (Psalm 1:3)

It is really very simple. It's not rocket science. How much easier can it get? It's not easy to do, but it is an easy concept to understand. Keep your distance from sin and take joy in doing what God says to do because you know his way is best. When you do these things, you will live a blessed, happy, prosperous life. You will be like a fruitful tree planted by a continual stream of water that is able to develop strong roots because it is properly hydrated.

Note that the psalmist says that you will be planted. Can you see outside from where you are sitting right now? If so, you may notice that there are two kinds of trees in your vicinity. Some grew naturally in their space. For example, some pine seeds blew out of a mature tree and randomly fell in the woods to later produce a new crop of pine trees. But some trees were planted in a specific spot. When a tree is planted, it is taken from one environment and placed in another that is more conducive to growth and stability. A planted tree is strategically placed by the gardener. The gardener decides where he wants the tree, and, by design, he intentionally sets it in just the right location.

Jesus said, "I am the true vine, and my Father is the gardener."[57] He promised that we would be fruitful as long as we stay close to him. When you keep your distance from sin and delight in God's teaching, God the gardener will plant you in the place you need to be in order to prosper. He will plant you in the right environment.

Where has God planted you? Do you have a stream of water nearby to give you spiritual sustenance? Do you have a group of fellow believers who help you in your spiritual development? Are you a part of a local body of Christ-followers who are serious about delivering the good news to all men and women? This is where you can develop strong spiritual roots. You grow and prosper in the faith when you team up with other like-minded believers who are dedicated to bearing spiritual fruit.

Is it in you to be a happy and blessed person? What will it take to get your spiritual life in order? What will it take to get your priorities in the right place? For many people, it is a matter of making time for your life with God and making time for your essential relationships, i.e., your family and your church family.

You can't be blessed if you don't take time to listen and obey God. You can't be blessed if you don't take time to spend with your family. You can't be a blessed parent if you don't take time to spend with your kids. Busyness keeps us from those most dear to us. In his book, *Bringing Up Boys*, James Dobson concluded that busy lifestyles are the primary reason for the breakdown of the family. Our children often suffer because of our busyness to make a living and to be prosperous in the world's eyes. But that's not what it's all about. One piece of fruit that God wants to bear in your life is a godly family.

Patrick Morley tells the story of Dr. Phil Littleford and his 12-year-old son Mark. They were on a fishing excursion with two friends in a secluded region of Alaska that could only be accessed by seaplane. They parked their aircraft and waded upstream to fish. Later that afternoon, when they returned to their camp, they were surprised to find the seaplane high and dry. The tides fluctuated twenty-three feet in that particular bay, and the pontoons rested on a bed of gravel. Since they couldn't fly out until morning, they settled in for the night and enjoyed some of their catch for dinner, then slept in the plane.

In the morning the seaplane was back in the water, so they cranked the engine and started to take off. They discovered too late that one of the pontoons had been punctured and was filled with water. The extra weight threw the plane into a tailspin. Within moments from liftoff, the seaplane crashed into the sea and capsized.

Dr. Littleford determined that everyone was alive. He suggested they pray, which the other men quickly endorsed. No safety equipment could be found on board - no life vests, no flares, nothing. The plane gurgled and submerged into the icy waters. Fortunately, they all had waders which they inflated.

They all began to swim for shore, but the riptide was strong. The Littleford's two friends were strong swimmers, and they both made it to shore. When the two men made it to shore, the last they saw of Phil and his son Mark was as a disappearing dot on the horizon, swept arm-in-arm out to sea.

The Coast Guard reported that they probably lasted no more than an hour in the freezing waters. Hypothermia would have chilled their body's functions, and they would go to sleep. Mark, with a smaller body mass, would fall asleep first in his daddy's arms. Phil could have made it to the shoreline, too, but that would have meant abandoning his son.

What father wouldn't be willing to die for his son? This heart-wrenching story illustrates the incredible love of a father. Every father reading these words would probably agree that they would do the same thing that Dr. Phil Littleford did for Mark. But my question is different. If we are willing to go so far as to die for our children, why is it that we aren't willing to live for them?[58]

Dads, it is not only important to live a blessed, happy, prosperous life for yourself. It is important for your kids. It is important for them to see you keeping your distance from sin and taking joy in being obedient to God. Be an example of what it is to be a blessed man.

Moms, are you so busy answering the tyranny of the urgent that you neglect the things that are most important? Do you spend more time actually enjoying your kids or transporting them in the mini-van from one activity to another?

Don't get so caught up in the noise and busyness of the culture. Don't get so consumed with your career, your house, your money, your hobbies, your cars...all of that stuff is going to burn one day.

When you live the kind of life described in Psalm 1, you will be fruitful. But the fruit and prosperity it talks about is not necessarily material things or money. It is about family and relationships. The fruit that you will bear when you are properly hydrating your life is quality relationships, a positive influence, and a servant's heart. That is what God wants for your life. It's not about things. It's about people.

For Discussion:

1. Can you recall a time in your life when you were desperately thirsty? Tell about it.

2. Do you have what it takes to live a blessed life?

3. How do you draw the line when it comes to influencing versus being influenced by those far from God?

4. Do you delight in God's teaching? If so, how can you help others do the same? If not, what can you do to make God's Word a delight for you?

5. Are you willing to die for your loved ones? Are you willing to live for them?

10

Getting Deep

"I want to go deeper."

"I wish my pastor would go deeper in his preaching."

"That church is shallow. They don't preach the whole gospel."

I've heard comments like these for years – especially since the contemporary church movement began a couple of decades ago. Contemporary and seeker-friendly churches are often accused of preaching a watered-down version of the gospel. Heavy on grace and light on sin. The promise of heaven but not a peep about hell. Liberal with love and little judgment.

Several times a year, someone will approach me and say, "Pastor, I want to go deeper." My response is usually, "What do you mean by that? Do you mean you want to get in over your head? That could be dangerous."

Common answers to what it means to be deeper seem to involve:

- End times theology, especially the book of Revelation
- Hebrew and Greek words
- Old Testament prophecy
- Expository preaching (text centered teaching style that expounds a passage as opposed to topic centered)

So what does it mean to live a deep Christian life? We may get all kinds of answers to that question. Maybe it helps to ask, "What is a shallow Christian?"

The Shallow Christian Life

A shallow Christian is one who claims to know Christ and who can point to a time in his life when he understood the basics of the gospel and internalized it and even publicized it (through baptism and church membership), but he has not taken the necessary steps to grow up in Christ. Instead, the shallow Christian has learned enough of the gospel to know how he should act in public but has no passion or desire to know Christ at an intimate and personal level. The shallow Christian fills a pew each Sunday. He serves, and even leads, some of the church's committees. He gives regularly to the church. He attends the church's special events and supports all the ministries of the church. He may even brag to his associates and friends about his church. He is a churchgoer, but he is not a "God-goer." He does not pray intimately much, if at all. He does not carve out time in his schedule to study his Bible. His efforts at personal and corporate worship are minimal at best. He makes little spiritual impact on those around him, and he has never personally shared the gospel with another person. He may know Christ as Savior, but he does not allow Christ to be Lord of his life. His life may be filled with church activities, but it is not filled with the Holy Spirit.

Sad but true. Our churches are full of shallow Christians. Each Sunday, church pews are occupied by millions of believers who have little or no interest in living a fully devoted life to Jesus Christ.

Hey! Maybe that is the definition of the deeper life. A life fully devoted to Jesus Christ. A passionate follower of Christ. Spiritual depth comes when you make loving and serving Christ your everyday mission. Going deep means living every minute of every day with the awareness that Jesus Christ is Lord and Ruler of your life. Getting deep means totally relying on, trusting in, and depending on God's Spirit to move and work in every area of your life.

There is no magic formula to living the deeper life. This is not something that you are going to accomplish by the time you finish reading this chapter. It is work. It is time-consuming. It is a lifestyle. It's a journey.

If you agree with me on what a shallow Christian looks like, then what does the deeper Christian life look like? What does the Bible say?

Searching for the Deep

The word or a form of the word "deep" occurs in the Bible 125 times. The large majority of those usages describe the depth of water, the depth of a building, or an emotion (e.g., deep love or compassion.) In the following verses, we find the word "deep" used to indicate that there is something more to knowing God.

> No eye has seen, no ear has heard, no mind has conceived what God has prepared for those who love him - but God has revealed it to us by his Spirit. The Spirit searches all things, even the deep things of God. For who among men knows the thoughts of a man except the man's spirit within him? In the same way no one knows the thoughts of God except the Spirit of God. We have not received the spirit of the world but the Spirit who is from God, that we may understand what God has freely given us. (1 Corinthians 2:9-12)

The Greek word for "deep" here is *bathos* which means profound, deep, or extent. The Amplified Bible translates *bathos* as the "profound and bottomless things of God - the things hidden and beyond man's scrutiny."

Note that it is not we who search the deep things of God but his Spirit. "The Spirit searches all things, even the deep things of God." But does this mean that the Spirit has to search to find out the mind of the Lord? No, the Spirit already knows the mind of the Lord. The Spirit does not have to study to learn the things of God. But the Spirit has come to dwell in us, and it is through him that we do the searching and the studying, and the Spirit of God opens the truth of God to us.

Therefore, we can only know the deep things of God by having God's Spirit live in us. We must live Spirit-filled lives in order to know the deep things of God.

The apostle Paul, the author of 1 Corinthians, explains why we have been given the Spirit of God. God's Holy Spirit is given to us so "that we may understand what God has freely given us."

Know the Mystery

Paul wrote another letter to Timothy, a young leader in the Church. In his exposition regarding church leadership, he uses another word for "deep."

Deacons, likewise, are to be men worthy of respect, sincere, not indulging in much wine, and not pursuing dishonest gain. They must keep hold of the deep truths of the faith with a clear conscience. (1 Timothy 3:8-9)

A different Greek word is used for "deep" in this letter. It is *musterion* which means mystery or secret. *Musterion* was often used to define a silent secret used during initiation rituals for a secret society or fraternity - like the Masonic Lodge, for example.

Again, the Amplified Bible translates it differently. They must possess "the mystic secret of the faith (Christian truth as hidden from ungodly men)" with a clear conscience.

In Old Testament times, there were great and wonderful mysteries that were kept hidden from men, even the prophets and priests. As enlightened as they were, they knew nothing of the many mysteries of God. They could not enter into the Holy Place. They couldn't imagine his sacrificial love. They didn't know the width of his mercy. They didn't fully comprehend his great grace. They lived during the preparation time - the time when God was preparing mankind for the Messiah - Jesus. Only until Jesus came on the scene can man begin to understand the deep things of God.

According to 1 Timothy 3, "to hold the deep truths of the faith" means to know the secrets of God. Don't you hate it when someone knows a secret, and they refuse to let you in on it? It is isolating and frustrating to not know what your friends know. You desperately want to be in on the secret, but your friend's lips are sealed.

What if I were to tell you that you can know the secrets of God? This is what it means to live the deeper life. How can we "hold the deep truths of the faith?" How can we live the deeper life?

E.M. Bounds wrote, "To be filled with God's Spirit, to be filled with God's Word, is to know God's will."[59]

If this is true, the first thing we must do, in order to go deeper in our walk with God, is to devote ourselves fully to the filling of God's Spirit in our lives. We must devote ourselves to the study of God's Word, and then we will be doing God's will. It is God's will that you "hold the deep truths of the faith."

The Old Testament prophet Daniel said God reveals deep and hidden things to us.

> Praise be to the name of God for ever and ever; wisdom and power are his. He changes times and seasons; he sets up kings and deposes them. He gives wisdom to the wise and knowledge to the discerning. He reveals deep and hidden things; he knows what lies in darkness, and light dwells with him. I thank and praise you, O God of my fathers: You have given me wisdom and power, you have made known to me what we asked of you, you have made known to us the dream of the king. (Daniel 2:20-23)

H.A. Ironside wrote,

> People say, "I do not know how it is that some folks get
> such wonderful things out of their Bibles. I do not get
> them out of mine. I know I ought to read my Bible, and
> I do read it, perhaps a chapter a day, but I do not have
> much appetite for it, I do not get much out of it." I will
> tell you why. It is because you do not sit down over
> your Bible in a self-judged, broken spirit, putting out
> of your life everything carnal, everything worldly,
> everything unholy, and then depending absolutely on
> the Holy Spirit who dwells within you to search into
> the Scriptures for you, to open the truth of God to you.
> God has given you the Holy Spirit for that very
> purpose. The Lord Jesus Christ said, "But when he, the
> Spirit of truth, comes, he will guide you into all truth.
> He will not speak on his own; he will speak only what
> he hears, and he will tell you what is yet to come"
> (John 16:13).

> Take a poor, simple, ignorant Christian who barely can
> read or write and put him down over his Bible in
> dependence on the Holy Spirit of God, and he will get
> more out of a given passage of Scripture in half-an-
> hour than a Doctor of Divinity or a Doctor of
> Psychology, who studies it with a lot of learned tomes
> about him depending upon his intellect instead of

upon the Holy Spirit. The Spirit of God opens the truth
to those who depend on him. I am afraid that many of
us are absolutely careless of the Holy Spirit who dwells
within us. We are trying to make our own way through
the world, trying to find out what is right and wrong in
spiritual things, instead of handing over everything to
the Spirit of God and depending on him to guide and
lead and unfold the Scriptures. He came to do this very
thing and he delights to fulfill this mission.[60]

So what does it mean to live the deeper life? It means
to know God's secrets. It means to know God intimately. It
means to know God to the fullest extent possible. It means to
allow God's Holy Spirit to search within us and for us to
discover the bottomless depths of God's grace.

How do you live the deeper life?

God's Cafeteria Line

When you go to a cafeteria, you're allowed to see and
smell everything on the menu. You can pick out exactly what
you want and leave those items that you don't desire behind.
The entire spread that the cafeteria has to offer is there for
your perusal. Your job is to scour the dozens of meats,
vegetables, salads, breads, and desserts and select a unique
plate that appeals to your appetite.

Many believers have treated Christianity like a cafeteria line.

Too many people have walked down the aisle of the church like they walk down a cafeteria line. They have looked at and studied the menu that Christianity has to offer, and they pick and choose what elements of the faith they want to have and they have ignored other elements. They have gone through the cafeteria line of faith and said, "Yes, I'll have some Jesus as Savior. I need to be saved. I don't want to go to hell. But, no, I'll pass on the Jesus as Lord. I don't want to get too serious. I still want to be in control of my life. I want to make my own decisions without God. If I need him, I'll ask for his help."

Later down the Christian cafeteria line, we consider our prayer life. "I know I should pray. I know that it's good for me. But I don't like it. I don't know how. I don't have time. I'll pass on prayer. God is good and he will bless me regardless. He's going to do things his way anyhow. Why should I pray?"

There's no way anyone could eat all of the food offered at a cafeteria. But God wants us to take all that he offers us. He enables us to handle all of the blessings that he can dish out. We simply need to humbly go to him and ask him to fill us with his Spirit, and he will give us his divine power that provides everything we need for life and godliness through our knowledge of him.[61]

We will never grow deeper in our relationship with God until we submit fully to him. This means we must recognize all that he has for us and receive all that he has for us.

In spiritual language, this is what is called Lordship. It is allowing Jesus to truly be Lord of your life. Let him be your boss. Let him be your Master. He made you. He created you. Don't you think he knows what is best for you? Don't you believe that his will for your life is far better than your will for your life? Since he loves you immeasurably more than you could ever imagine, don't you know that he will provide you with more blessings than you could ever dream? It's true. He is Lord, and when he is Lord of your life, his will falls into place for you like a trail of breadcrumbs for one lost in the wilderness.

Submit Yourself Humbly to God

> If my people, who are called by my name, will humble themselves and pray and seek my face and turn from their wicked ways, then will I hear from heaven and will forgive their sin and will heal their land. (2 Chronicles 7:14)

It is a promise of Scripture that when we humbly submit ourselves to God, he will bless us immensely. There are four conditions and three promises made in this verse. We must be humble. We must pray. We must seek God's face, and we must turn from our wicked ways. When we do these four things, he will hear us. He will forgive us, and he will heal us.

Note that the very first thing we must do is humble ourselves. Before prayer, before seeking God's face, before turning from sin, humility is required. Prayer is weak when pride is present. This is why most of our prayer postures indicate humility. Have you ever wondered why we bow our heads before we pray? It is an act of humbling ourselves before our Maker. When we bow our heads, kneel, or lay prostrate before God, we are humbling ourselves in his presence.

But humility is more than just an act prior to prayer. It is a lifestyle. It is an attitude. It is a character trait found in those who have a deep spiritual life.

If you study Christian history, you will find that the movers and shakers in the kingdom of God were very humble people. For example, George Mueller, a great man of faith and prayer, rescued approximately 10,000 orphans during his lifetime. Mueller never asked men for help. He trusted God to meet the daily needs of the ministry even when the cupboards were bare, and he had no idea how he would provide the next meal to his boys. Mueller's story is one of incredible faith and selfless service. It is a reminder of what one fully surrendered life can accomplish when it is humbly submitted to God.

Dedicate Yourself to Prayer

Oswald Chambers wrote, "The great enemy to the Lord Jesus Christ in the present day is the conception of practical work that has not come from the New Testament, but from the systems of the world in which endless energy and activities are insisted upon, but no private life with God."[62]

The second condition in 2 Chronicles 7:14 is to pray. Learn how to pray. Read classic books on prayer. Learn different ways to pray. Discover prayer walking or journaling. Put a classic prayer to memory like the Lord's Prayer, the prayer of Jabez, or a Psalm. Join a prayer group or find a prayer partner who will hold you accountable.

We allow the busyness of life to cheat us out of quality prayer time. Our calendars, gadgets, and inability to sit quietly to pray and meditate on God allow the gap in our relationship with him to increase. Bill Hybels authored a book titled, *Too Busy Not to Pray*. It was titled with Martin Luther, the key figure of the Protestant Reformation, in mind who once said, "I have so much to do, that I cannot get on without three hours a day of praying."

We naturally think just the opposite of Luther. We maintain a lifestyle with no margin, little downtime, and constant interruption. We are too busy to pray. Luther understood that the busier he was, the more he needed to pray. He recognized that when he worked, he worked. But when he prayed, God worked.

I confess that I have been aggravated at believers who tell me, "I don't have time for prayer. I don't have time to read my Bible. It's difficult for me to find time to spend with God." Then, when the subject is changed that same person rattles on and on about every show they watched the night before on primetime television. We have the time. We just have to make prayer a priority.

Eating the Elephant

Only a small percentage of people can say they have read the entire Bible. It is an intimidating proposition even for the most avid reader.

Don't be demoralized by the size of the Bible. How do you eat an elephant? One bite at a time. Learn the basics before you try to dig too deep. Some people try to go straight to the book of Revelation before they understand anything else. Can you read the last chapter of a novel and understand what the whole book is about? No. So don't start with the last segment of the Bible.

If you are new to the Bible, start reading about the life of Jesus in the Gospels, the first four books of the New Testament. The book of Mark is a short synopsis of Jesus' life. Read Mark, then move on to Matthew, Luke, and John. After that, you may want to read the first two books of the Old Testament. The book of Genesis lays a foundation for the rest of the Bible. Much of what you read in the Bible goes back to

Genesis. There will be some puzzling things that happen in Genesis, but read through it and get to know it. The book of Exodus is Moses' record of the nation of Israel escaping slavery from Egypt. Like Genesis, foundational stories and principles are laid out in Exodus.

From that point, you may want to go back to the New Testament and read more about the creation of the Church and the challenges it faced in its infancy. The books of Psalms and Proverbs are always full of inspiration and wisdom. You can visit those books frequently. They are favorite books among millions of Bible readers throughout the generations.

One mistake Bible readers frequently make is to think that it has to be read in order. While this is certainly fine and profitable, it is not necessary. The books of the Bible are arranged based on category and/or author. They are not in chronological order, i.e., the order in which they were written. For example, all of the books of the Law written by Moses are placed first in the Old Testament (Genesis through Deuteronomy). The historical books are next (Joshua through Esther). The poetic books (Job through Song of Songs, a.k.a., Song of Solomon) come next, and the prophetic books are last (Isaiah through Malachi).

There are many books available that can help you navigate your way through the Bible. You may want to find a Bible handbook or a reference book that can help you eat this elephant!

If you're pretty familiar with the Bible and looking for a fresh way to approach it, learn how to do a word study. For example, study all of the instances of the word "deep." Here's your chance to get into the Hebrew and Greek words! You can also focus on a specific topic or person in the Bible.

The Bible is a life-long textbook. It is like no other book because it provides fresh insights even when it is read every day. The most important thing, however, is to act on what it says. Most believers throughout Christian history had no chance to read their own copy of the Bible. Not until the Gutenberg Press was invented in the 15th century was it even available to laymen – if they could read! Even today in countries where the Bible is banned, Christ-followers smuggle in copies of God's Word - sometimes one page at a time – for believers who desperately want to read it. Yet even in times when Christ-followers didn't have their own personal copy of the Bible, they were fruitful because they acted on what they knew it said.

We live in a time when the Bible is available in various translations and paraphrases. It can be read and studied in many formats, on the internet, and even on our cell phones. For Americans, we have easy access to the Scriptures. It is a shame if we do not take advantage of it.

The Classics Rock

The best sellers list at your local Christian bookstore has good books. But most of the popular Christian books today will be forgotten tomorrow. The writings of the latest and hottest teachers, pastors, and authors will be on the shelves of your nearest Goodwill store in a few years. They may speak to you today, but in a few years they will seem to be irrelevant. But there are some works that will never grow old. They are classics. There is a reason why these books are timeless. They have spoken to generations of believers over the years. They have moved Christian leaders to new heights.

I want to encourage you to read more than what is hot off the shelf. Read the classics. Classic authors on the deeper life include Andrew Murray, E.M. Bounds, Hannah Whitall Smith, Watchman Nee, Charles Finney, G. Campbell Morgan, C.S. Lewis, R.A. Torrey, Oswald Chambers, John Stott, Peter Lord, Jack Taylor, and Jamie Buckingham.

Read about great Christians of the past like George Mueller, William Wilberforce, or William Tyndale. See how God worked in their lives. Watch how they grew in their faith. Study their attitudes toward life, the world, materialism, time management, the church, and God.

Worship is Not a Spectator Sport

Have you ever wondered why the thing that churches do on Sunday mornings is called a worship service? Are we really worshiping? And who are we serving? Unfortunately, too many churches have become spectator events rather than participating events. The crowd watches and listens to a choir or a band sing to the Lord. When the congregation is invited to participate, many reluctantly stand and turn their hymn books to the appropriate page or look at the lyrics on a video screen with a blank stare.

You know it's true.

Worship is not a spectator sport.

Going to watch a football game is not the same as playing in a football game. Going to a movie is not the same as being in the movie. Watching a parade is not the same as participating in the parade.

Just because you attend a worship service doesn't mean you worship. It's easy to stand and watch singers on stage worship. It's easy to clap and sing and enjoy the music. You can do that at a Bon Jovi concert. But it is quite another thing to worship.

A worship service is a designated time when a body of believers can gather to serve God through worshiping him corporately. You serve God when you worship him. You worship God when you serve him. You worship God through giving. Observing worship is not fruitful. Worshiping realigns, refocuses, and refreshes our outlook on God and life. Worship brings us back to center. Worship lifts up Jesus Christ who said, "When I am lifted up from the earth, I will draw all men to myself."[63]

When you worship, you lift up Christ. When you lift up Christ, those around you see him and are changed by him. When you sit and stare, there is no life. When you participate, even with a "joyful noise," you bring life to others.

Learn how to make worship personal. Don't allow it to be a spectator sport. Take advantage of opportunities in times of corporate worship to genuinely participate with other believers in lifting up praise and thanks to God. You can worship alone too. Make opportunities for personal worship during your quiet times with God and when listening to music around the house or in the car. Don't be an observer of worship. Be a true worshiper.

Don't Get in Over Your Head

If you want to get deep, don't jump in over your head. I was surprised and pleased to find that Oswald Chambers, a deep Christian thinker and one of my spiritual mentors, wrote about the value of shallowness and the dangers of depth. Chambers reminds us that God works in the shallow aspects of life equally as much as the profound. "We sometimes refuse to be shallow, not out of our deep devotion to God but because we wish to impress other people with the fact that we are not shallow. This is a sure sign of spiritual pride."[64]

We make an impact on those around us not with our Bible knowledge and profound thinking but with the character and content of our lives. The shallow things of life, i.e., working, eating, conversing, recreating, are ordained by God just as much as church meetings, Bible studies, and Christian living classes.

Make a commitment to yourself and to God that you will progressively do more, learn more, serve more, give more, and love more as a passionate follower of Jesus Christ. The Christian life is not a sprint, it's a marathon. Love God with all of your heart, soul, mind, and strength, and love your neighbor as yourself. Obey God like a dutiful child obeys their father. Give your life to Christ, hear his Word, and put it into practice.

That's deep.

For Discussion:

1. Prior to reading this chapter, what was your idea of going deeper spiritually?

2. Are you guilty of strolling down God's cafeteria line and choosing only the things you want from him instead taking all that he offers you?

3. Who is a great example of humility to you? Why?

4. Making time for prayer and Bible study are basic disciplines for followers of Christ. Why is it such a struggle for so many believers?

5. Are you a participant or a spectator at worship? How do you make worship personal?

11

When God Comes Quickly

In September 1857, a 49-year-old businessman named Jeremiah Lamphier,[65] had a heart for New York City. He distributed flyers and visited boarding houses, shops, and offices inviting people to a prayer meeting at the Old Dutch North Church on Fulton Street in Manhattan. The church was dying. The neighborhood was in transition. Other churches left the neighborhood, but the leaders of Old Dutch North were determined to stay where the church had been for the past eighty-eight years. Jeremiah Lamphier quit his job to work for $1000 a year to make visits on behalf of the church. It was slow. A few people came as a result of his work, but it was very discouraging, and he quite often grew weary. Many times he cried out to God and humbly asked God over and over again to give him strength for his mission.

The idea occurred to him that businessmen might want to seek refuge for a short period of prayer once a week during the lunch hour. Lamphier began to advertise and invite people to the weekly prayer meetings.

On September 23, 1857, at noon, Jeremiah Lamphier sat in an empty room and waited for people to come and pray. Ten minutes passed. Then another ten minutes. No one came. Finally, ten minutes later at 12:30, Jeremiah heard someone approaching the room. Then another man came and another. Soon there were six men who came to pray. They prayed and discussed the need for prayer. They concluded that there should be another meeting the following week and agreed to meet then.

Twenty men came to the next meeting. The next week, there were forty. Jeremiah Lamphier decided that there was a need for daily meetings in a larger room.

On Wednesday, October 14, 1857, the stock market crashed. Banks closed. Men were out of work and families were hungry. The prayer meetings were now called the Fulton Street Prayer Meetings, and they filled not only the larger room but the entire building. In a matter of weeks, over 3000 people of all backgrounds and professions filled the church daily for prayer. By January 1858, there were at least twenty other prayer meetings going full tilt in the city. Within six months, 10,000 New York City businessmen, out of a total population of 800,000, were gathering everyday for prayer. Newspapers were sending reporters out to write stories about the great happenings as a result of the prayer meetings. "The

Progress of Revival" became a standing column in the papers as reports of God's blessings were printed.

News began to spread about revival throughout the Northeastern United States. One man arrived at the Fulton Street prayer meeting with a handbill advertising the meeting. He said that he received it while standing on the banks of the Mississippi River over 1000 miles away.

Soon cities like Philadelphia, Boston, and Washington, D.C., reported citywide revivals and prayer meetings. At least 150 towns in Massachusetts were moved by revival with over 5000 conversions before the end of March 1858.

The revival fires spread throughout the Northeastern corner of America over the Appalachians and to the West. Every major city felt the power of this sweeping revival – Cleveland, Cincinnati, Detroit, Indianapolis, Minneapolis, Chicago, St. Louis, Omaha, all the way to the Pacific Coast.

The revival moved south as well. Southern Methodists added 43,000 members during the revival period. At its peak, it was determined that 50,000 people were converted per week. One million people were saved in 18 months. Church membership increased dramatically, and thousands of marriages and families were miraculously restored.

One Chicago newspaper said the effects of the national revival were apparent to everyone and seen in every walk of life. The merchants, the farmers, the mechanics, everyone was living a better, more orderly and honest way of life. A product of the Chicago revival was a shoe salesman named Dwight

Moody. Moody took some boys off of the street and began a Sunday School class. It was the beginning of a ministry that lasted over 40 years and impacted people around the globe.

Why did this happen? It happened because one man humbled himself to pray for his church, his city, and his country. It happened because Jeremiah Lamphier believed 2 Chronicles 7:14. He humbled himself and prayed. It happened because one man chose to slow down the busyness of his life to pray. It happened because one man chose to follow God rather than money.

Can God do it again? Of course. He is the same yesterday, today, and forever.

I believe that God wants to send revival again - a revival that will sweep through your city and mine. He can and he will if only we will humble ourselves and pray. I believe that God is just waiting on us to act.

I have been fascinated with revival and spiritual awakenings for many years, and there is a lot that can be said about them. Numerous books have recorded incredible stories of God bringing 180 degree changes in individuals, communities, and continents. Now, don't let the word "revival" fool you. I'm not talking about heavy-handed preachers in a week-long series of services. I'm not talking about the scheduled fall or spring revival meetings that your church might have each year. I'm talking about a spontaneous, God-sent, Spirit-induced spiritual awakening not manufactured by men but anointed by God. True revival comes as a surprise to most and is prayed down by a few.

A Sudden Surprise

In both the Old and New Testaments, when God brings his glory down in a unique and awesome way, he does it suddenly and unexpectedly. Even devoted followers are caught off guard by the instantaneous grace and mercy of God. Unbelievers are often gripped with fear and astonishment. One scholar said, "Revival is God springing a convicting surprise on his creation."

Note the sudden surprise on the Day of Pentecost:

> When the day of Pentecost came, they were all together in one place. Suddenly, a sound like the blowing of a violent wind came from heaven and filled the whole house where they were sitting. (Acts 2:1, 2)

God came quickly in Isaiah's day too. He said to stubborn Israel, "I foretold the former things long ago, my mouth announced them and I made them known; then suddenly, I acted, and they came to pass."[66] God worked quickly in this case against hard-hearted Israel. When God chooses to move among his people, he often does it in a hurry.

In revival history, the effect of the sudden work of God is very striking. Those who are far from God – who have not prepared themselves for an encounter with the Almighty or even thought about spiritual things – will suddenly be overwhelmed with conviction of their sin. The great evangelist and revivalist Charles Finney wrote that when God was moving in a community, there were times when strangers to the spiritual events around them who happened to be nearby would instantly be smitten with conviction of their sin and converted to Christ.

During the 1857 Revival in America, it was reported that crews on ships were overcome by the glory of God as they drew near the ports where revival was taking place. Ship after ship arrived with the same talk of sudden conviction and conversion. A captain and his entire crew found Christ at sea and arrived at their port rejoicing in what God had done in their midst. This sudden and spontaneous overwhelming sense of God bringing deep conviction of sin is one of the most amazing and outstanding features of true revival.

What is behind this swift movement of God? Obviously, it is the sovereignty of God. But it is also known that, even though few people are aware of it, you can be sure that there has been someone like a Jeremiah Lamphier "standing in the gap"[67] and praying constantly for God to move among his people.

Honesty

When awakening comes, people get honest with God and each other. It usually involves a combination of three things: repentance, prayer, and unity. Beginning with the great revival in Acts 2 and following revival history throughout, we discover that spiritual awakening comes when men repent of their sin, have a burden for prayer and communion with God, and live together in love and harmony.

Revival happens when men begin to realize their position in God's eyes. When people are genuinely awakened to the seriousness of their sin and God's awesome holiness, repentance comes. We find in Exodus 33 that the people of Israel had become disappointed with God and their leader Moses. They began to blaspheme God and told Aaron to make a golden calf that they could worship. God said that he would withdraw his presence from them. Soon they were arrested by the severity of their sin and drawn to repentance. Every record that has been written about any great spiritual movement of God in the history of God's people has this common theme: an overwhelming awareness of sin and the urgent need for repentance.

On October 31, 1517, in Wittenberg, Germany, Martin Luther took the first steps toward what is now known as the Protestant Reformation by posting his famous ninety-five theses on the church door. In those days, the church door served as the community bulletin board. This is where news, announcements, and upcoming events were posted. Luther began a newsworthy event when he posted his God-led convictions. "When our Lord and Master Jesus Christ said, 'Repent,' he willed the entire life of believers to be one of repentance," Luther wrote along with his theses. His brave and outspoken behavior led to the consciousness of the abuses of the Church - its leaders and members. The Church was in a sad state of affairs. She had become a place of idolatry, selfishness, spiritual apathy, and overall lack of concern over sinful practices. Martin Luther awakened the Church to the holiness of God, the gravity of sin, and the importance of faith.

When true repentance takes place, prayer and unity follow. When men and women see the severity of their sin and witness the holiness of God, they respond by getting right with God through prayer and getting their relationships right with people through love and unity.

Do we realize the difference in the powerful Church we read about in the New Testament and the Church today? Do we realize God's displeasure with our churches? Why has it been so long since our country has experienced a mighty move of God? Why is it that a true Great Awakening has not been experienced in America since the 19th century? Why has it been so long? Why are things as they are? Why is the Church counting for so little? Why is she so ineffective? Why do 3000-4000 churches close their doors each year in this country? Why do thousands of churches add not one person to the Kingdom of God each year? Why is it that men and women are living in sin with no regrets and no remorse? Why can't revival come to our land today?

In order for God to move in a mighty way in our church, we must realize the seriousness of our sins and have a deep awareness of the position we find ourselves in. When we come to terms with God's great dissatisfaction with our sinful lifestyles and realize that even on our best days our righteous acts are like filthy rags,[68] then we will face the facts that we cannot continue to live like we have been living, and we will repent and turn from our old way of living. We will develop a passion for spiritual things. We will engage in spiritual conversations. We will worship God sincerely, serve him obediently, give generously, and live abundantly.

A Universal Awakening

When revival comes, it affects people of all classes and, therefore, spreads like wildfire among all types of individuals. When spiritual awakening comes, people of all ages, races, socio-economic groups, and educational background are blessed. It is not confined to religious people. God gets everyone's attention whether they are looking for him or not. During the 1735 Revival that began with Jonathan Edwards in New England, it was recorded that, "There was scarcely a single person in town, either old or young that was left unconcerned about the greater things of the eternal world."

Those who were the most vain and those who lived life loosely were affected. Those who were most likely to make light of it all were saved. At least 50,000 people were added to the churches of New England out of a population of 250,000.

An Overwhelming Consciousness

Another characteristic of revival is an overwhelming consciousness of God. For example, the sailors who felt the presence of God so strongly – even before they made port. When God chooses to bring revival, he moves in every life and makes all aware of his presence. The book of Acts describes people who "were cut to the heart" when they heard the gospel.[69] A few verses later it says, "Everyone was filled with awe, and many wonders and miraculous signs were done by the apostles."[70]

When Jonathan Edwards preached his famous sermon *Sinners in the Hands of an Angry God,* it wasn't the power of Edwards' presentation that moved the congregation; it was the presence of God. Jonathan Edwards was not a flamboyant preacher. There were no gestures, no shouting, and no drama in his preaching style. He was near-sighted. He read with his manuscript just inches away from his face and made no eye contact with his audience. He delivered his message in a monotone voice. He used one and two syllable words that everyone, even children, could understand. He never talked about himself, only the Bible and illustrations from nature.

But God's power was in his preaching. As Edwards preached, the congregation bent over with a devastating conviction of their sin. They understood that their relationship with God was in a precarious position. They felt as though they were on the very edge of the abyss into a Christ-less eternity. There was such distress, moaning, and weeping that Edwards had to ask them to be quiet so that he could be heard. People were gripping the pillars of the church and the sides of the pews as though they already felt themselves sliding into the pits of hell.

Charles Finney said that while preaching in New York during the Great Revival, the presence of God was so strong that many in his congregation fell from their seats and cried for mercy. He wrote, "If I had a sword in each hand, I could not have cut them down as fast as they fell. I was obliged to stop preaching."

When revival comes, the power of God is so strong that he cannot be resisted even by the hardest of hearts. The rankest of sinners gives God their attention when his presence is so awesome. Everyone is filled with awe and wonder at the glory of God. I believe that we need a movement of God again in our churches, in our cities, and in our nations. Pray with me that God will bring revival to our land. That is how revival will come; we must pray.

J. Edwin Orr, a renowned scholar and authority on spiritual awakenings, said that prayer is the key. "We must pray, then God will work." Matthew Henry said, "When God intends great mercy for his people, he first of all sets them to prayer." Remember 2 Chronicles 7:14, "If my people, who are called by my name, will humble themselves and pray, and seek my face, and turn from their wicked ways; then I will hear from heaven and will forgive their sin, and will heal their land."

Coming Out of a Slump

Not many people realize that America went through a significant spiritual slump after the American Revolution. Drunkenness and profanity were an epidemic. Women were afraid to go out at night. Bank robberies were a daily occurrence. Churches were losing ground. The Methodists were losing more members than they were gaining, and the Baptists and Presbyterians were stagnant. Some ministers reported that they had not had a convert in as much as 16 years. The Lutherans were considering joining the Episcopalians, and the Episcopal Bishop of New York got another job because there was nothing for him to do.

John Marshall, the Chief Justice of the United States, wrote that the Church was "too far gone to be revived." It was predicted that Christianity would be forgotten in 30 years.

They took a poll at Harvard and discovered that there were no believers in the student body. Princeton found two. They had anti-Christian plays at Dartmouth and burned

Bibles in campus bonfires. Christians were so few on college campuses that they met in secret.

In 1794, twenty-three New England ministers, led by a Baptist pastor named Isaac Backus, sat down together to consider the spiritual condition of their country. The effects of the Great Awakening of 1735 had obviously worn off.

The ministers agreed on one thing – a revival was desperately needed. "What shall we do about it?" they asked themselves. The only answer: pray.

They issued a "circular letter" calling on church people to pray for revival. They were specific. Let there be "public prayer and praise, accompanied with such instruction from God's Word, as might be judged proper, on every first Tuesday, of the four quarters of the year, beginning with the first Tuesday of January, 1795, at two o'clock in the afternoon and so on continuing from quarter to quarter, and from year to year, until, the good providence of God prospering our endeavors, we shall obtain the blessing for which we pray."[71]

Apparently hearts were hungry, for there was an enthusiastic response. All over the country, little praying bands sprang up. In Ohio, Kentucky, and Tennessee, "covenants" were entered into by Christian people to spend a whole day each month in prayer plus a half-hour every Saturday night and every Sunday morning.

Seminary students met to study the history of revivals. Church members formed "Aaron and Hur Societies" to hold up the hands of their ministers through intercession.[72] Groups of young men went to their knees to pray for other young men. Parents prayed for their children's conversion.

The stage was set. What happened as a result of this concerted prayer effort has gone down as the most far-reaching revival in American history.

What happened? Not long after that, revivals and spiritual awakenings were being reported from small towns throughout New England. Meeting houses were filled night after night as towns were turned upside down for God. Many college campuses were changed during the Second Great Awakening.

Jonathan Edward's grandson, Timothy Dwight, became the president of Yale College in 1795. Yale was antagonistic toward Christianity. Timothy Dwight challenged the students to discuss if the Bible was truly the Word of God. Most of them argued against the sovereignty of the Bible but with shallow, invalid arguments.

Timothy Dwight began a series of lectures including his most famous 1796 sermon titled "The Nature and Danger of Infidel Philosophy." Almost immediately, the student body of Yale was spiritually transformed, and it set the stage for four more revivals on the campus over the next few decades.

Outside of New England, camp meetings and circuit riding preachers were instrumental in bringing revival. Cane Ridge, Kentucky, played host to what must have been the largest revival meeting ever in early American history. Attendance estimates were anywhere from 20,000 to 30,000 people. Preachers of all denominations were spread out among the people preaching four to five at a time. As the Holy Spirit moved among the crowds, hundreds of people were swept down in moments of humility and worship.

During this period of revival, church membership multiplied, new denominations were formed, and the modern missionary movement began. The American Bible Society was a result of revival, and the Sunday School movement took off. The second Great Awakening led to the abolition of slavery, the women's suffrage movement, and the establishment of public education.

Dwight L. Moody said, "Every great movement of God can be traced to a kneeling figure."[73] It has happened before; it can happen again, if we will pray.

For Discussion:

1. What comes to mind when you think of revival?
2. Have you ever experienced true revival? How did it happen and what happened?
3. Why is it so important for Christ-followers to get honest with God and others?
4. What would happen in your church if a few people prayed intensely for a spiritual awakening?

12

The Main Business
of Your Life

I mentioned my inventor grandfather's perpetual motion machine earlier. Perpetual motion is defined as movement that goes on forever. A perpetual motion machine would move continually and produce more energy than is put into it. Many people have attempted to develop such a machine but with no luck.

When I read 1 Thessalonians 5:17, I think of perpetual motion. "Pray continually." The King James Version of the Bible says, "Pray without ceasing."

This brief command haunts many people. We hear this short verse and wonder how it is possible to pray all of the time. We can't pray 24 hours a day. We have to concentrate on other things like work, our family and friends, household chores, eating, and other responsibilities of life. How can you pray continually? Is it possible to be a perpetual praying machine?

It's a relief to know that the word "continually" in the Greek does not refer to perpetual prayer. It does not mean that we are to literally maintain a posture of prayer at all times. The word "continually" means frequent, regular, or habitual. In Biblical times, this word was used to describe a hacking cough that never seems to go away.

Paul, the author of this annoying verse, was encouraging us to maintain continuous fellowship with God as much as possible in the midst of daily living. Someone paraphrased this verse "Make prayer the main business of your life."

With a few exceptions, Christ-followers have never taken prayer seriously. Only a handful of believers take it seriously today. For the most part, prayer is like a meaningless trinket that sits on a dusty shelf in your home. It's only purpose in life is for decoration. For many people, prayer is a salve used to sooth the conscience; a ritual mumbled before a meal; or a word used to express concern for someone – "Our prayers are with you." We pray sometimes not about decisions to be made but to make us feel better about decisions already made.

We are not very good prayers. We don't make prayer the main business of our lives. We're not sure what good there is in prayer. If God is a sovereign God who does what he desires, when he desires it, will my prayers really have any impact? Won't he see that his will is done regardless of my prayers or lack of? Who am I to ask God for anything? I have no credibility with God.

John Wesley said, "God does nothing except through prayer." S.D. Gordon said, "The greatest thing anyone can do for God and for man is to pray. You can do more than pray after you have prayed, but you cannot do more than pray until you have prayed."

It is every believer's responsibility to pray. The Church has been given the charge to make prayer the main business of our lives. Let me explain why.

Our Struggle is with Spiritual Powers

> For our struggle is not against flesh and blood, but against the rulers, against the authorities, against the powers of this dark world and against the spiritual forces of evil in the heavenly realms. (Ephesians 6:12)

Though it sounds like something from Hollywood or a Steven King novel, it is not. The Bible tells us that evil spiritual beings under the direction of Satan swarm the earth in an attempt to foil and frustrate God's people. They are constantly inciting rebellion against God and his purposes. The war that began in heaven when Satan was thrown out has not ended. It only changed locations. The battle continues here on earth.

These "spiritual forces of evil" seek to control governments, leaders, influencers, and even the Church. Moral failures, criminal acts, and military conflicts are the result of the enemy's activity and influence.

By God's own design, this unseen activity operating in our world is kept in check by one thing and one thing only. These evil spiritual forces are not controlled by armies, navies, or police. They are not subject to guns, bombs, planes, or tanks. By God's own choice and by God's own making, the only power that controls these evil powers is the power of God's Holy Spirit which is released by believing prayer.

We Have Been Deputized

All authority in heaven and on earth has been given to me. Therefore go and make disciples of all nations, baptizing them in the name of the Father and of the Son and of the Holy Spirit, and teaching them to obey everything I have commanded you. And surely I am with you always, to the very end of the age. (Matthew 28:18-20)

When Jesus had called the twelve together, he gave them power and authority to drive out all demons and to cure diseases. (Luke 9:1)

Jesus gave his authority to the disciples several times. The passages above are just a couple of instances of this transaction taking place. But the disciples were not the first ones to be given authority over Satan. In Revelation 12, when Satan and his followers were ejected from heaven, it was not the personal intervention of God that forced him to earth. God deputized Michael and his angels.

> And there was war in heaven. Michael and his angels fought against the dragon, and the dragon and his angels fought back. But he was not strong enough, and they lost their place in heaven. The great dragon was hurled down - that ancient serpent called the devil, or Satan, who leads the whole world astray. He was hurled to the earth, and his angels with him. (Revelation 12:7-9)

The same power that was given to Michael and his angels was given to the Church. Just as Michael and his angels were deputized with authority in heaven, so Christ-followers have been deputized with authority on earth.

But our problem today is that rather than being a powerful, confident presence in prayer as God's strong deputy, the Church is more like Barney Fife – weak, feeble, and frail. Although all authority belongs to Christ alone, he chooses to exercise his authority through the prayers and faith of his Church. We are the hands and feet of Christ. We enforce God's authority on earth.

We Influence World Affairs

If it is true that our struggle is against spiritual powers, and if it is true that we have been given the authority of heaven, then this explains why prayer should be the main business of our lives. This is why John Wesley said, "God does nothing except by prayer."

The praying Christians of the world hold events of the world in the palm of their hands. If you were to survey the people in your town today and ask, "How much influence does the Christian Church have in this world?" what would be their response? Some? A little bit? Not much?

Would the people you surveyed believe you if you told them that the prayers of the Church actually determine human events?

Some day we will discover that prayer is the most important factor in shaping the course of human history. When the history books of heaven are opened, it will be written that the real molders of world events were not kings, presidents, prime ministers, Senators, governors, or mayors but prayers.

In those same heavenly history books, we will find out that history was not made in the Oval office, the Pentagon, the

Senate, the House, or Parliament. History was determined in the secluded prayer closets of believers around the world.

Think about it. The movements of men and nations are initiated and inspired in the spiritual realm. The spiritual realm is influenced and controlled by the power that is released by the prayers of God's people. The fate of the world is in the hands of nameless, praying saints.

By making prayer the main business of his life, the least-endowed, least-known person in the world may become greater in God's history book than the most brilliant and most famous person in the entire world who fails to pray.

We need to understand that we do more by our praying than by our service. It doesn't matter how articulate you are, how intelligent you are, how helpful you are, or how compassionate you are; you are poorly equipped to serve in God's kingdom if you do not pray.

Why? Because Ephesians 6:12 says so. We are in a spiritual battle. We are not fighting against humans. The only power that is effective in this world is the power of the Holy Spirit who, by his own design, is liberated and released by the prayers of God's people.

Our struggle is with spiritual powers.

We have been deputized with the authority of heaven.

We have a tremendous influence on world affairs.

Someone Doesn't Want You to Know

Since these things are true, Satan will do all he can to keep you from praying. He does not want you to comprehend the power of prayer.

His most successful strategy to weaken a pastor is to keep him so occupied with committees, church events, hospital visits, sermon preparation, benevolence calls, counseling, and putting out fires that flame up every day that his spiritual life is starved.

Satan's most successful strategy to weaken a church member is to keep you so occupied with business, housework, yard work, committee meetings, social events, playing taxi driver with the kids, sports activities, email, and television shows that your spiritual life is starved.

As long as the enemy can keep you busy and distracted from your prayer closet,[74] he will be satisfied. Activities have their place - even church activities are great. But they cannot take the place of prayer.

Does this mean we are to pray and nothing else? No. But we must pray first. Prayer sets the stage for service. S.D. Gordon said, "Prayer is striking the winning blow. Service is gathering up the results."

If we do not pray, there is no fire.

I use God's mighty weapons, not those made by men, to knock down the devil's strongholds. These weapons can break down every proud argument against God and every wall that can be built to keep men from finding him. With these weapons I can capture rebels and bring them back to God, and change them into men whose heart's desire is obedience to Christ. (2 Corinthians 10:4, 5 LB)

Don't let roadblocks that the enemy puts in front of you keep you from praying. "Greater is he that is in you than he that is in the world."[75] We cannot be distracted, intimidated, or overcome by the enemy. We have the authority and the ability to pray revival into our churches, our communities, our counties, our state, and our country. It happened with the prayers of Jeremiah Lamphier and a few others in New York City. Why can't it happen again?

Make prayer the main business of your life. Learn how to pray selflessly. Remember that prayer is not reaching for things in the hand of God. It is reaching *for* the hand of God.

For Discussion:

1. Do you think Christ-followers take advantage of the power of prayer? Why or why not?

2. What do you think about spiritual warfare? Is it real to you or does it seem far-fetched and weird?

3. If you were to survey the people in your town, how much influence would they say the Church has in the world?

4. Did this chapter encourage you, challenge you, or upset you? Why?

5. What can you do today to make prayer the main business of your life?

13

What the World
Needs to Know

Ted Turner changed the world at five o'clock in the afternoon on Sunday, June 1, 1980. The Cable News Network (CNN) went on the air as television's first ever broadcast of the latest news 24 hours a day, seven days a week. Before then, Americans relied on the radio for the latest news updates. If there was a major news event, CBS, NBC, and ABC would interrupt regular programming. Otherwise, you would have to catch the local news at 6:00 or 11:00 PM or the network news at 6:30 PM. Of course, newspapers were a major source of information, but you had to wait until morning to get yesterday's news.

In the days of the famous Walter Cronkite, the network news shows had thirty minutes each weekday evening to tell you what was happening in the world. With

CNN, the news would be available anytime. It was truly a life-changing event. When the world needs to know something, it can turn to Ted Turner's network for the answers.

Obviously, the way we receive news has changed even more in the 21st century. Today I can pull up the news, weather, and sports, plus more on my cell phone while I'm walking my dog. The internet has made the gap between a news event and its delivery into your home or hands almost instantaneous. When you need to know something, it is ready and waiting for you.

Jesus wants his followers to deliver his good news. It's one of the main purposes of our lives. We are designed to share his amazing grace with others. He has commissioned us to go and tell his life-changing story.

Why don't we just do what Ted Turner did? Let's just broadcast it on television for the whole world to see.

Been there. Done that.

The problem with Christian television is that non-Christians don't watch it. Shoot, Christians don't watch it much unless they are homebound or in prison. Unfortunately, too many of the hucksters on Christian television cause people to resist God's grace rather than embrace it. Sometimes I wonder if Christendom would be better off if we shot down all of the Christian TV satellites out in space.

The Christian TV industry would insist that they are spreading the good news in a remarkable way. I have to admit,

I have actually met one person in my life who became a Christ-follower as a result of watching *The 700 Club*. One.

In some people's minds, it is worth the billions of dollars spent on satellites, towers, cameras, lights, staff, etc. for that one soul.

I would suggest that it is poor stewardship.

The internet has created a new way to spread the gospel of Jesus Christ too. While it may be too early to tell, all indications are that it is a more effective way to share the good news, but there are still lots of problems and challenges that come with web evangelism.

So if the world needs to know about Jesus and if broadcasting is not the answer, what is the best way to get this news delivered? How do we communicate Jesus to our world? What should be communicated about Jesus? What exactly does the world need to know?

The answer to "how" is relationships. Someone once said that evangelism is one beggar telling another beggar where to find bread.

Television, radio, computers, and books will always be formats for sharing the gospel of Christ, but the best and most effective way for the world to learn about Jesus is through a genuine, honest, one-on-one relationship.

Jesus told us to make disciples in his Great Commission.[76] It's hard to make a disciple without knowing the person. You can't baptize someone through the airwaves.

Teaching is more effective when it is done in person, not via satellite or DVD.

Changing the world requires relationships. Mass evangelism methods only work effectively when Christ-followers are present with non-believers to answer questions and engage in personal conversation when the big event is over. Web presentations of the gospel are great, but it is even better when someone presents it live and in person. Chat rooms and message boards are being used by missions organizations today to reach people around the globe through their PCs and Macs, but isn't it more effective when you can look a disciple in the eyes?

If the world is going to discover Christ, Christ's people have to be in all corners of the globe in relationship with the world's citizens. It's just that simple.

Once we have established a relationship, what do they need to know?

Jesus Is Real

In 1997, I was awarded an all-expenses paid trip to the Holy Land. It was incredible. I highly recommend going there if you ever have the chance.

"But, Gene, isn't it dangerous over there?"

Could be. We heard Israeli jets bombing the Lebanese border less than twenty miles away when I was there. When we asked our Israeli tour guide if we should be concerned, he waved it off and said, "Nah, it just goes with the neighborhood. The last thing they'll do is bomb a bus full of Americans."

Among the scores of amazing things I witnessed there, one of them was the knowledge of our Jewish tour guides. These men made a comfortable living showing Christians around Israel. They had no doubt in the historical figure of Jesus Christ. They showed groups where he was born, where he taught, where he performed miracles, where he died, and where he was resurrected. The guides knew and quoted New Testament scriptures better than this ordained Christian minister. They believed that Jesus was a great man, teacher, and prophet, but they did not believe that he is the Messiah.

The evidence and life of Jesus was right in front of their eyes almost every day, but they didn't grasp the reality of Christ.

I know a lot of good ole boys in the Bible Belt that think the same way. They've attended church. They've attended Sunday School. They show up for Christmas and Easter services. They believe in Jesus. They just don't believe that he is for them. They don't really think that Jesus has anything to do with every day life. They think he's a crutch, a life raft, or someone to "accept" at the last minute on their deathbed, just in case.

The world needs to know that Jesus is real. Paul wrote, "Reality is found in Christ."[77]

How are people convinced that Jesus is real? When Christ-followers commit themselves completely to him. When they see Jesus really working in our lives.

It's what changed me.

I grew up as a good ole Bible Belt boy. I'd heard of Jesus. I never doubted his existence. I knew he had some good teachings, but all of that religious stuff just wasn't for me. At least, not until I met some people who had an encounter with Christ that they couldn't shake off. They allowed Jesus Christ to be central to everything they did in life. They were devoted to him. He was real to them. They claimed him as their best friend. They weren't religious nuts either. Yes, they were involved in their local churches and attended regularly, but there was no religiosity; only a reality that they could not deny.

As my relationships with my new friends grew, my understanding of the reality of Christ swelled. I was soon changed and I was transformed by a real and living Savior. It was because my friends showed me that Jesus is real.

The world will know that Jesus is real when they see him real in your life. You don't have to act like a religious zealot. You don't have to be kooky. You don't have to speak King James English. You don't have to carry a big, black Bible everywhere you go. You don't have to call everyone "brother" or "sister."

Be yourself. Within the context of your life and within your God-given personality, show Jesus to be real in your life.

When those around you see him really operating in your life, they will know that he's real.

Jesus Is Relevant

Do you know anyone who struggles with sin and temptation? Do you know anyone who needs hope and encouragement? Do you know anyone who would like supernatural wisdom and instruction for every day life?

If so, then Jesus' teaching is for today. His words are as relevant today as ever. The world needs to know that Jesus is relevant. His teaching has contemporary application for us today.

> All Scripture is God-breathed and is useful for teaching, rebuking, correcting, and training in righteousness so that the man of God may be thoroughly equipped for every good work. (2 Timothy 3:16)

Do you know anyone having financial problems? Jesus taught more about money than anything else. Do you know anyone who desperately needs to have more love in their life? Jesus taught all about it. Do you know anyone who needs more wisdom? Jesus is full of it. Do you know anyone that wants to know more about what happens when we die? Jesus can tell you.

Jesus taught volumes about the things that men and women have wondered about and needed help with for generations. His teaching is as relevant today as it was in the first century.

We only have a glimpse of his teachings in the Bible. In fact, John recorded in his gospel that the world cannot contain all of his teachings![78]

Jesus is not irrelevant. I think it is a sin to let Jesus appear irrelevant! I believe this is one reason why approximately 80 percent of American churches aren't growing. They've made Jesus irrelevant to the culture. They are still singing songs about Jesus to an organ when everyone else is singing to electric guitars. Ministers stand stiffly behind pulpits wearing a robe while the culture is in jeans and t-shirts. We're guilty of speaking "Christianese" and leaving the unaffiliated at a distance. Our Christian culture has its own subculture that sometimes makes it impossible for outsiders to get in. Too many of our churches are like the Titanic. They are slowly sinking, and no one wants to believe it.

The world needs to know the relevance of Christ. Show them.

Jesus Is Reliable

Whom can you trust these days? Too many things are unreliable today. You can't rely on technology. Hard drives never warn you before they crash. You can't always rely on your employer. Ask the millions of Americans who recently received a pretty pink slip from their boss. You can't rely on politicians. Seems a crooked one has his mug shot in the morning paper at least once a month. You can't rely on organizations. They falter and fail due to man's imperfections. Don't assume that your investments are safe. Who knows when Wall Street will come tumbling down? We can't wake up today expecting the same peaceful world that we experienced yesterday. September 11, 2001, taught us that lesson. Some people can't even rely on their parents. Their own flesh and blood betray them.

There is one who is always reliable, always trustworthy, and always faithful. A psalmist wrote, "From birth I have relied on you, you brought me forth from my mother's womb. I will ever praise you."[79] The writer understood that he relied on God even before he was aware of God.

The Bible is full of stories of people who learned to rely on God. From Genesis to Revelation, God's people discovered that he could be trusted. Whether it was in the midst of a flood, slavery, war, or natural disaster, God proved himself reliable. Jesus said, "He who sent me is reliable."[80]

Jesus - God in the flesh - showed us that we can rely on him. Everything he said he would do, he has done. For those things he has yet to accomplish, we can trust him because his record is unblemished, and his word is true.

We live in an unstable world. We don't know what tomorrow will bring. We don't know what the future holds, but we know who holds the future. Men will let you down, but Jesus will never let you down.

The world needs to know that.

Jesus Is Our Redeemer

Someone gave me a coupon for a free ice cream cone. My wife and I are terrible about using coupons and gift cards. They typically sit in a drawer in our kitchen until they expire. Fortunately, I remembered the free ice cream coupon one night. When I had a craving for a frozen treat, I took the slip of paper out of the drawer and drove over to the store. I ordered my dessert and instead of taking cash for payment, the cashier accepted the coupon that said I was allowed one free ice cream cone. I redeemed my coupon.

We don't use the word "redeem" much in our everyday language. Unless you are redeeming a coupon, redeeming a mortgage, or redeeming your microwave from the pawnshop, it's just not a word we often hear. Redeem has several meanings, mainly, to buy back, exchange, or convert something of value. It also means to make up for defects or to set free from an undesirable state.

Jesus is our redeemer.

Jesus has redeemed you from the defects in your life. He has redeemed you from an undesirable state.

Everyone was born with a birth defect – a spiritual birth defect called sin. Since the days of Adam, men and women were born with a natural bend toward selfishness. That's all sin is – selfishness. All sin can be traced to our self-centeredness. Jesus Christ has redeemed us from the birth defect of sin. He redeems us from all wickedness.[81] In Christ, "we have redemption, the forgiveness of sins."[82]

Jesus made the great exchange. He exchanged his life for ours when he took on the sin of the world at the cross.

Not only has he redeemed us from sin, Jesus redeemed us from the law.[83] Living according to the law, legalism, is a performance-based religion. Jesus has set us free from the curse of the law. God doesn't accept us based on our performance. He accepts us based on his grace. You are totally accepted, totally forgiven, and totally loved by God!

What exactly is the law? The law includes all of the religious rules, beliefs, and traditions that man has created to "help" people try to please God. Living by the law focuses more on your performance and good deeds rather than God's grace shown on the cross.

How do you know if you are living according to the law? Here's a little quiz that might help you.

Suppose you were to rate yourself on a scale of 1-10 in comparison with other Christians as you think God would rate you. Do you believe that you rate as high as your pastor? What about Billy Graham? Would you rate yourself up there with Mother Teresa? The apostle Paul? What about Jesus Christ?

If you answered any of these questions no, you're focusing on your performance instead of grace. We think God accepts us based on our deeds. Too many Christ-followers think they have to live the perfect Christian life in order to be loved and accepted by God.

You are as righteous and acceptable in the sight of God as your pastor, Billy Graham, Mother Teresa, the apostle Paul, and even Jesus Christ himself. Look at Paul's words:

> God made him (Christ) who had no sin to be sin for us, so that in him we might become the righteousness of God. (2 Corinthians 5:21)

Read that verse again slowly. In fact, go get your Bible and underline it. Then memorize it. Jesus Christ, the perfect sacrifice, became sin on your behalf so that you could have the righteousness of God. This means that when God sees you, he sees you as totally forgiven, totally accepted, and totally loved. God looks at you just as he looks at Jesus - clean, pure, perfect, righteous, holy, and loved. He sees you just as if you've never sinned. That's what the word "justified" means – just as if you've never sinned.

Jesus has redeemed you from sin, and he has redeemed you from the law. You don't have to give in to sin any longer. You don't have to try to perform your way to heaven. You're in! If you are a follower of Christ, you simply follow – even if it means you stumble along the way at times.

Jesus Christ has done it all for you. All you have to do is follow him.

God's grace is amazing because he has done all of the work. You don't have to work your way into heaven. Jesus has paved the way for you. We are totally forgiven, totally accepted, and totally loved by God not because of anything we have done but because of everything Christ has done for us.

Christianity is a "want to" faith, not a "have to" faith. Too many people that think they have to do this or that to win God's approval. They think Christianity is a matter of following the rules, obeying a dress code, getting perfect attendance in Sunday School, and being perfectly groomed.

I follow Christ because I want to, not because I have to. Miserable Christians (and those that make others miserable) are typically those who are so busy complying to the law and policing other Christians' actions that they have forgotten about grace. They are caught up in following all of the religious rules. This is a terrible testimony of what the cross is all about.

The cross gives us freedom. The cross allows us to do whatever we want, but because of God's grace, we choose to follow him. Maybe the story of the city dog and the country dog will help make this clear.

I have a city dog named Deacon. Deacon likes to follow his nose and ramble around our neighborhood freely, so we can't let him outside the house without a leash. Sometimes we put him on a chain in the backyard that is anchored to the ground. When he visits my in-laws, he can run around freely in their fenced in backyard. But very rarely is he able to go outside without some kind of restriction such as a leash, chain, or fence for fear that he will run away.

A country dog, on the other hand, may live on 500 acres with the freedom to roam and run wherever he pleases. But when you drive up to the country dog's house, where do you typically find him? Lying on the porch. He is waiting for his master to pet him or play ball with him. He's close to his master because he wants to be there, not because he is bound there by a leash, chain, or fence.

As a follower of Jesus Christ, you are like the country dog. You have all the freedom in the world. You can roam and ramble through the countryside. You can choose to go astray, or you can choose to stay close to your master. You are not like the city dog bound with restrictions. You have liberty to do whatever you wish. But because you want to avoid sin and breaking the heart of God, you can choose to stay close to him.

When you have a rich relationship with Christ, you'll want to maintain that relationship and delight in everything that God provides for you. You will understand that to choose to go astray with sin is foolish but to stay close to the Master is wise.

This is why Jesus redeemed us - so that we could enjoy and cherish our relationship with him. The world needs to know this.

The world needs to know that Christianity is not about following rules, but it's about following the Savior. The world needs to know that it's not about performance. It's about grace. The world needs to know that Jesus has set us free from sin and the law and that we live in the sight of God totally forgiven, totally acceptable, and totally loved by him.

That's why it is called amazing grace.

Your job is to go and let the world know that Jesus Christ is real, that he is relevant, that he is reliable, and that he is our redeemer. When God asks you to do the impossible, laugh like Sarah and press on. When you mess things up, remember that God gives "do-overs." When you're tempted by greed, give thanks for what you have. When you feel powerless, remember that you're God's dynamite box, designed to carry his power. When you need to be stretched, go deep. When you start your day, pray. When you end your day, pray. As you go through your day, pray. Stay close to Christ like the country dog stays close to home because you want to be close to your Master.

This is your purpose. This is your commission. Go and be blessed.

For Discussion:

1. Why don't people take the reality of Jesus seriously?

2. How has Christianity made Jesus seem irrelevant?

3. Do you have many reliable friends? Who are they? What makes them reliable?

4. Do you believe that God sees you just as he sees Christ? Is this news to you?

5. Are you a country dog or a city dog?

Notes

[1] Steve Brown, *Servant Magazine*, September, 1993, p. 8
[2] 2 Peter 3:18
[3] Exodus 8:8-12
[4] James 4:14
[5] 2 Corinthians 5:17
[6] Matthew 28:18
[7] Isaiah 64:6
[8] Philippians 4:13
[9] Philippians 3:12
[10] Matthew 28:18-20
[11] Luke 6:12-13
[12] Mark 1:16
[13] 1 Corinthians 1:26-2:5
[14] 1 Corinthians 1:27
[15] 1 Samuel 16:1-12
[16] 1 Corinthians 1:30
[17] Ibid.
[18] 2 Corinthians 10:10
[19] 1 Corinthians 2:4,5
[20] See pages 48-49
[21] Matthew 13:44
[22] Matthew 25
[23] Proverbs 2:5
[24] Colossians 3:3
[25] A. W. Tozer, *The Pursuit of God* (Camp Hill, PA: Christian Publications, 1982), pp. 19-20
[26] Genesis 18:10-12
[27] Hebrews 11:8-12
[28] Genesis 18:14
[29] Exodus 15:11
[30] Judges 13:17-18
[31] Luke 1:36-37
[32] John 12:24
[33] John 3:3
[34] Hebrews 11:6
[35] Daniel 6:16
[36] Matthew 8:1-4
[37] Matthew 8:14-15
[38] Matthew 9:18-26
[39] Matthew 9:27-31

40 Mark 8:22-26
41 Luke 7:11-17
42 Matthew 14:13-21
43 Matthew 14:22-33
44 Luke 22:21
45 Luke 22:49-51
46 Matthew 27:46
47 Luke 23:46
48 1 Peter 3:18
49 Hebrews 10:31
50 John 10:27-29
51 The Bible has many verses about eagles. Isaiah 40:31 is probably the most popular one.
52 2 Corinthians 5:9
53 See the King James Version of this verse.
54 Matthew 5:6
55 Revelation 2:4-5
56 Hebrews 10:32
57 John 15:1
58 Patrick Morley, *The Man in the Mirror* (Grand Rapids: Zondervan, 1997), pp. 116-117
59 E. M. Bounds, *The Best of E.M. Bounds on Prayer* (Grand Rapids: Baker Book House, 1981), p. 18
60 H. A. Ironside, *1 Corinthians* (Neptune, NJ: Loizeaux Brothers, 1972), pp. 97-98
61 2 Peter 1:3
62 Oswald Chambers, *My Utmost for His Highest* (New York: Dodd, Mead & Co., 1935), 293 (October 19 entry)
63 John 12:32
64 Oswald Chambers, *My Utmost for His Highest: An Updated Edition in Today's Language* (Grand Rapids: Discovery House, 1992), November 22 entry
65 Some records spell Jeremiah's last name, Lanphier
66 Isaiah 48:3
67 Ezekiel 22:30
68 Isaiah 64:6
69 Acts 2:37
70 Acts 2:43
71 *America's Great Revivals* (Minneapolis: Dimension Books), p. 27
72 Exodus 17:12
73 E.F. and L. Harvey, *Kneeling We Triumph: Book One* (Hampton, TN: Harvey and Tait, 1982), 9

[74] A prayer closet is a term that was derived from the King James Version of Matthew 6:6.

[75] 1 John 4:4

[76] Matthew 28:18-20

[77] Colossians 2:17

[78] John 21:25

[79] Psalm 71:6

[80] John 8:26

[81] Titus 2:14

[82] Colossians 1:14

[83] Galatians 3:13; 4:4-5

About the Author

Gene Jennings has been a pastor since 1987 having served churches in Texas, Georgia, and South Carolina. He has traveled as a missionary and speaker in many other states as well as Australia, Tanzania, Mexico, Costa Rica, and Guatemala. Gene is the Associate Pastor at TrueNorth Church in North Augusta, SC. He is a graduate of the University of South Carolina-Aiken and Southwestern Baptist Theological Seminary. He lives in North Augusta with his wife, Beth, and their dog, Deacon, and cat, Napoleon. He has one son, Cliff, and one daughter, Bailey.

Gene blogs at www.genejennings.com. He is also the author of *Timely Words*.

You can email Gene at genepjennings@aol.com.

If you enjoyed *Laughing with Sarah*, please visit www.LaughingWithSarah.com and buy one for a friend.

Thanks!